POSTBOX
KASHMIR

2017

PEN ON PAPER

Have you ever written a letter? Stared at a sheet long and hard, smoothened an imagined crease, made the momentous decision of writing from the first line or second. Picked a pen and stopped again. Is it 'dear' or 'dearest', is the date on the top right, top left or somewhere at the bottom? Then smiled, turned around on the bed, flat on your back, eyes facing the ceiling, thinking once more about what follows: 'dear' or 'dearest'. Taking your time, twisting the pen in your fingers, before turning back on your stomach, resting on your elbows, facing the blank sheet of paper yet again. After all, it is a letter. Where each letter forms careful words strung together with quiet deliberation.

Am I romanticizing letter writing? Maybe. Acts assigned to memory often carry nostalgia. And old letters a sense of history. Movement of time. An archive of experiences, feelings, opinions. Felt deeply enough to be penned on paper.

I've only ever written letters to my friends and my lover. It was sweet. The act of writing. Followed by the act of waiting. Slow and full of anticipation. Just like the care it took to organize my thoughts, select and reject what I wanted to share, as I assessed how much I wanted to bare my soul. Once it left my desk and dropped with a quiet definitiveness into the dark insides of a red postbox, I lost all control. There was no delete, no backspace, no recycle bin.

In a few hours, it would be picked by a postman (I don't think I have ever seen a postwoman), who would probably cycle to the nearest post office and add it to a stack of bank statements, bills, invitations, consequential and inconsequential advertising, special offers and other letters. Of promises, dreams and heartache. Unique, when they were written, with care and specially apportioned time. And ordinary, when they lay there, to travel across cities via postal vans and mail trains as life went by as usual.

It could be a couple of weeks or more before I heard back. There was the time of travel and then there was the composition of the reply. The waiting as delicious as the writing. Letter for a letter.

But slow communication is no more a thing. Life is lived in the moment via social media. Questions are followed by reactions, followed by comments, sometimes followed by trolling—all happening very quickly. It all feels extremely significant in that moment until the next viral moment swoops in and swiftly makes the previous obsolete.

Apps are designed in a way that messages and photos only stay for a limited time before disappearing, leaving no mark, no history. Responses are expected to be instant and those taking longer than usual can be tracked via blue ticks. Questioned, often shamed for not being within reach. There simply isn't enough time. The fear of missing out keeps us on our toes. Communication has a different pace, and it is more urgent than ever.

So, it is likely that some of you have never written a letter, except for a school assignment or for a friend's birthday. Duaa and Saumya hadn't. Until in the summer of 2017, when they became part of a BBC project—to share their lives from Srinagar to Delhi and back.

It probably began in the summer of 2016, but then it is hard to say when it all really began. Kashmir remains in the subconscious of most of us, particularly of journalists. Like a simmering pot of milk, most times on a slow flame but one slip of attention and it boils up and spills over.

Wars have been fought for complete control of the former state of Jammu and Kashmir (now the two union territories of Jammu and Kashmir and Ladakh). It is claimed in full by both India and Pakistan, but both govern parts of it. China has control of eastern Kashmir's Aksai Chin, won after defeating India in the 1962 war. In 1989–90, a long-festering armed rebellion against Indian rule gained popular support in the Valley, strengthened with the rise of Pakistan-backed militant groups and the Indian armed forces had to be deployed in the state. The forces were given additional authority and special immunity to deal with the challenge. The 1990s also saw the minority Kashmiri Hindus being targeted by militants in the Valley. Tens of thousands have died in clashes since, including militants, security forces and civilians. Cross-border infiltration and militancy have been brought under control, but protests for self-rule erupt regularly. Kashmir remains one of the most militarized zones in the world.

After strained relations for almost a decade with Pakistan, the new century saw peace gestures between the two countries. There was a decline in militancy. Though the armed forces were still omnipresent in the Valley.

A new generation was born, one that had no experience of the volatile 1990s. Including two young women, Duaa in Srinagar in 2002 and Saumya in Delhi in 2001.

But it was only an uneasy calm. The pot had been simmering. A churning in the minds of those who were born during the 1990s. A decade before the new millennium. Before Duaa and Saumya. Before a semblance of peace had started taking shape. They had witnessed encounters, disappearances and slogans for self-rule as they went to school. Now they were teenagers. Stepping out of a tense childhood. Taking tentative steps into an uncertain adult life.

Seventeen-year-old Tufail Ahmed Mattoo was studying in Class XII in the summer of 2010. One afternoon in June, he was hit by a tear gas shell fired by security forces deployed at an anti-India demonstration in Srinagar. He died almost instantly.[1] Mass protests erupted. Angry mobs of young men confronted security forces. Their weapon of choice: stones. More than a hundred people, mostly youth, died in the clashes. And hundreds were jailed for stone pelting. And this was not the first summer of protests, deaths and violence; the previous two years had seen a similar cycle. Fuelled in 2008, by a controversy over the transfer of forest land to the organizers of the Hindu pilgrimage, the Amarnath Yatra and in 2009, by allegations of rape and murder of two women by security forces.[2]

Kashmir's challenge now came from within. Discontent and anger against the government and the armed forces, spilling on to the streets in the form of stone pelting. Boosted by those seen as the new 'heroes'. It was termed a new wave of militancy that was spreading, in part, by social media. And a young militant leader became the champion of their cause.

Born to a highly educated upper-class Kashmiri family, Burhan Muzaffar Wani did not hide. Photos of him and his associates openly brandishing AK-47 rifles, videos in which he kept his face unmasked, started getting widely circulated via YouTube, Facebook and WhatsApp. Boys started dropping out of school and college to take up guns. His message spread fast through the these popular online communication tools and were debated in Kashmiri homes as they broke bread together in the traditional dastarkhwan.[3]

It was summer again. In 2016, Ramazan, the month of fasting, had just concluded and Eid festivities were still in the air. One Friday, the leisurely evening quiet was shattered. The pictures first emerged on social media: bullet-ridden bodies of Burhan Wani and two of his associates, killed in an encounter with the security forces.[4] And the images spread like wildfire.

The Valley boiled like never before. Stone pelters were back on the streets and even pellet guns did not deter them. Wani's funeral was attended by tens of thousands. Clashes erupted. The youth, again, against the security forces. And the numbers piled up. Estimates ranged from about a hundred deaths to more than 380 in the year 2016.[5]

The pictures captured the passions as they came into our office in Delhi. I was now working as a correspondent with the BBC. We watched the summer stretch into autumn as the Kashmir Valley witnessed the worst unrest since the insurgent 1990s. My journalist colleagues on the ground and in Delhi spent months reporting on the politics, the policies and the people affected, bringing in the perspective of the government and the governed. Yet in our office, there was a feeling that something was still missing. The Kashmir 'problem' as it was widely referred to, needed more humanity—a step back to delve deep. It also needed to tell the story of those writing its destiny at that moment. Many editorial brainstorms later, we found our answer: teenagers.

To capture the impact of the geopolitics, we needed to step away from it. From the action on the streets back into the quiet of homes. We wanted to understand Kashmir from the perspective of the young minds growing inside it, and to explain it to the young generation watching it from the outside.

This generation was smart and curious. They had been born with a smartphone in their hand and had information at the swipe of a finger. They talked less, typed more. Half a billion Indians now had access to the internet, with the majority in urban areas.[6] Social media, most popular among the youth, was becoming as common as email. In fact, in 2017, India overtook the United States to become the country with the largest user base on Facebook. And half of those people used it as a source of news.[7] Then, there were platforms like Instagram and Snapchat, where words were almost immaterial; the pictures did the talking. Socializing, whether intimate or communal, was now taking place in the virtual world.

We needed to listen into their conversations. Who were they talking to? What were they talking about? In this hyperconnected space, was the world really their oyster or were algorithms constructing their ecosystems? How much did a young girl growing up in the country's capital Delhi know about the life of a girl in one of the most militarized zones in the world? Did adults dictate that knowledge? And was it clouded by the noise they lived in, online and offline?

There could be no definitive answers. But there was a counter-intuitive thought. About going back to the basics, peeling off layers to get to the bare bones. The message was what we wanted to discover, but the medium was equally vital. What if our teenagers disconnected completely? What if they did not see each other or know anything about each other? What if they started from scratch and made a fresh connection—by writing letters? Careful, slow and deliberate.

I was going to look for two teenagers, one in Srinagar and the other in Delhi, to ask them to become pen pals. And then the BBC would publish their letters opening up a conversation between those in Kashmir with those outside it.

They had to be girls. Equally impacted but less expected to be the tellers, characters or readers of writings about conflict. If we were to tell the story of unseen Kashmir, why not choose the unexpected?

This was part of a wider thinking shaping up within the BBC—an attempt to bring a gendered lens to our storytelling by choosing women to tell them. Historically, men have been the writers and readers, and by default, most writing has captured the lives of men. Arguably, women's experiences are documented less, especially in the context of issues that are not specifically about them. Women appear as mothers, wives, daughters, survivors of sexual assault, carers of the elderly, even teachers but not as the average student, the unemployed, the business owner and probably not as the ordinary young person living through a conflict. We believed that would be a different, nuanced perspective. That is why they had to be girls.

They had to be young. When the mind is less rigid, still open and forgiving. Experience brings maturity but also a certain firming up of opinions. We didn't want politicized beliefs but personal experiences.

They had to be comfortable with agreeing to our request to not look each other up on social media. To keep the anonymity of the interaction as true as possible. Whether the letters got sent via post or email, the experience of being pen pals needed the distance.

And this was no writing contest, but they had to be fond of putting pen to paper. And then happy with giving up their private conversations to the world. I was asking for their trust and since they were still underage, through their parents.

Finding my letter writer in Delhi was a pleasant accident. I hadn't really started looking at that time. On a completely different mission, one winter afternoon in February 2017, I found myself at Saumya's house. It was books that led my husband and me there. Both of us, he way more than me, are guilty of hoarding books. And now, a carefully built selection of over fifteen years needed a new purpose. Our search for a library, where we could part with our much-loved treasures knowing they will be equally valued, was what led us there.

It was a cosy unassuming two-bedroom flat in a colony in outer Delhi. Saumya's parents ran a small library-cum-reading room from an even smaller space on the floor above. They could have rented it out to supplement their income, but decided to use it to work with schoolgoing children by providing them a place to come read. As the name suggested, Umang Library was to spread the simple 'joy' of immersing in the written word, to give wings to young imaginations. We were inspired with what we saw and went back down three floors to make multiple rounds, heaving cartons full of books up a narrow, broken staircase.

Saumya didn't speak much at that time. She quietly helped with the unpacking and laying out of books, stopping only to peer at some titles from behind her thick spectacles. She was fifteen years old and preparing for her Class X board exams. We didn't talk about Kashmir.

A few weeks later, when I started the search for my letter writers, I recalled the shy young girl from that winter afternoon. The more I thought about it, the more she seemed to be the perfect fit. A couple of phone calls later, it was done. Saumya Sagrika was waiting to get her first letter.

In Kashmir, the situation was very different. I had never been there, I had no family there and very few friends. As I started making calls, finding connections and building bridges to reach out to parents, it became very clear that the biggest hurdle was going to be trust. It was the casualty of decades of conflict. Entering into anyone's circle of trust is always difficult, but on some days, it seemed unsurmountable. The physical distance, lack of confidence that a personal meeting could build, all added to the challenge.

In 2017, there were visible strains of pain and anger. The violent autumn after Wani's encounter had quietened as snow covered the streets in the Valley. But the cold seeped in through the telephone line from the other side when I tried to explain our project. The memories were very raw. There was a strong belief that the momentous upheaval led by young people was going to change something. The rage was still simmering. At that time, when opinions, borders and beliefs had a razor-sharp edge to them, my offer of a quiet conversation over letters seemed suspiciously innocuous to the parents on the other end of the phone call.

But I persisted, not losing hope. Days turned into weeks, which turned into months. And finally, a door opened just a crack. My request had landed at fifteen-year-old Duaa's doorstep, with just a recommendation from an acquaintance trusted by her family, holding this together.

Duaa's father had a gentle demeanour. We discussed the project a little and then some more. But we spent a lot of time trying to know more about each other. Me and my family and Duaa and hers. The conversations with her parents were never rushed and always began with courtesies that extended to my parents, my husband and his family. This was my lovely introduction to Kashmiri *tehzeeb* (etiquette). As trust grew, the anxieties became more honest too. And some stemmed from what had happened to another Kashmiri teenager.

Sixteen-year-old Zaira Wasim was the young star of the hugely successful Bollywood film, *Dangal*, released in December 2016.[8] In January, when she returned to her hometown, Srinagar, and got photographed with then chief minister Mehbooba Mufti, it caused a storm on social media. Zaira was criticized for the photo op; people said she should have met victims of pellet gun firing instead. Some saw it as taking sides. Was she for the government and against the protestors? Or could this just be an innocent gracious acceptance of appreciation? Zaira Wasim issued an open letter with an apology via her Instagram handle. She later deleted it but not before it got widely reported in national news media. Zaira did get support too, many pointing out how young she was, but the fine line that needed to be treaded in Kashmir, even by a teenager, just became even more thin.

When I was growing up, my mother introduced me to the idea that 'personal is political'. The slogan, which has its roots in the feminist movement, has stayed with me. That our personal lives cannot be alienated from our politics. And that our personal life inside our home, has a political context. For a journalist who has to always work hard to be balanced in her writing, this acute political consciousness has been sobering as well as illuminating. A challenge one has to rise to every time.

In Kashmir, this slogan takes a much deeper hue, the shadow of which can be unsparing. Duaa's mother feared that her daughter would not be able to walk the tightrope. Or that what she wrote, could get lost in translation. We gave ourselves some more time, a few more conversations. And a promise that we would publish whatever her daughter wrote, without any editing. Because we believed we had chosen with care. I imagined it as a teenager's diary, hoping to find an unbridled innocence and honesty. It was a give and take. I was putting my faith in them and they were giving me their trust. Eventually, I got an invitation to stay with them in their house whenever I planned to visit Srinagar. It was a sign, they were ready.

In April 2017, Duaa Tul Barzam wrote her first letter to Saumya Sagrika.

This is their story.

Srinagar
25 April 2017

Dear Saumya,

A very warm and pleasant salaam from a place known to be heaven on Earth—Kashmir. I'm Duaa Tul Barzam I know, long name, but you can call me Duaa). I'm a fifteen-year-old studying in one of the most prestigious institutions of India—Presentation Convent School. I'm a simple girl from a simple family but a wonderful one. I'm a part of a nuclear family in which my hero my father (Baba), my beautiful mother (Mumma), my naughty nine-year-old brother (Aveen) live with a strong family bond. I have a lot of friends and by 'lot', I mean a lot, but still my BFF are Ayra (Chutki), Fatima (Fatty) and Liqua (the sarcastic one). They are the reason my school life is really cool. I'm sure you must be knowing the meaning of friends in one's life and you must be having your besties with you disturbing you all the time like mine (they just can't leave me alone).

You must be curious about Kashmir. As I already said, it is heaven on Earth. We have really chilly winter months and warm summers. It's so chilly here that the chilliest winter months are called *chil-e-kalan*. We have really good and beautiful tourist spots like Pahalgam, Sonmarg, Yousmarg and the winter king—Gulmarg, just to name a few. I have visited all these places, but it was my first time this year to see the winter king—Gulmarg. The way it is originally supposed to be seen with snow, snow, snow everywhere. Can you even imagine—about 7-feet-high snow everywhere around you, taller than you? There were many winter sports organized by Government of Jammu and Kashmir in Gulmarg this year. Although I'm not a sports person, my brother Aveen is. He even got the first position for his basic technique in skiing and honestly I was completely taken aback by this news because until last year he thought skiing is boring.

You must be interested in some sport? I would like to know about the sport that you play.

As I mentioned, I'm a simple girl. A simple girl who likes to read, write, dance, annoy my brother, listen to music. And mentioning about music, I must tell you that I'm a big music freak. I'm inspired by Western and Kashmiri music, which is soothing and when the instruments like tumaknari (a sort of dhol) and nott (a big steel vessel played with keys) are played in harmony, they make you wanna get up and dance like a crazy person. At times the lyrics are heart-touching, at times they are so funny, actually hilarious (trust me you want to laugh the whole time if you are listening to a funny Kashmiri song). I also love Western music, mainly pop, alternative pop and rock, R&B. I love artists like One Direction (although they are currently on a hiatus), Little Mix, Zayn Malik, Selena Gomez and Justin Bieber (by the way I'm really happy he is coming to India). You must be thinking I'm crazy telling you about my music interest, but I feel the music that I love will tell you more about me than I ever can. I also sing a bit in my free time (not professionally, of course) but my mom tells me to shut it down every time I sing in front of her. She can't bear it (actually nobody can).

I hope you liked my letter and you will reply to me soon.

Until next time,
Duaa

PS: I am attaching a picture of a snow sculpture carved by Kashmiri youth this year during Gulmarg snow festival. I really hope that you will like it.

Delhi
28 April 2017

Dear Duaa,

I got your letter and am very happy to know that you are also a fan of One Direction! Let me introduce myself first. My name is Saumya Sagrika. I am fifteen years old and live in India's capital Delhi. I have a small and wonderful family. There are only three of us, me, my mother and my father. I don't have any siblings, but there is a five-year-old in my neighbourhood and he does not let me feel the absence of a brother. Samarth troubles me just like a younger brother. In fact, he divides my mother and father's love in two parts. I study in a school very close to my house. I have a lot of friends in school who hold a lot of importance in my life. I'll tell you about my best and closest friend, Palak (she is very thin so we call her 'Piddi'). You asked me about my favourite sport, so I'd like to tell you that that is taekwondo. I have won a silver medal at a state-level championship also.

If I were to tell you about myself, then I'd say that I'm very different from other girls (that's what I think). I just don't like to dress up like other girls. In my free time, I like to read books and listen to music just like you do.

Like I mentioned that I live in Delhi, I'd like to tell you that the weather here is very unpredictable. Sometimes it's too sunny, on other days, it rains heavily. I wish the weather here would also be like Kashmir!

I wanted to share one thing with you. Here, whenever people hear anything about Kashmir, the one word that comes to their mind is 'Muslim'. I want to know if it's true that only Muslims live there.

I know you must be feeling that I am jumping from one thing to another, but what do I do, I have to say many things to you.

Hope you liked my letter and will reply soon.

Saumya

Srinagar
3 May 2017

Dear Saumya,

Received your letter and I'm glad to know that you are a reader and a music listener like me. Well, to be more specific, a Directioner like me.

In your letter you asked me a question that whenever the people outside Kashmir hear anything about the Valley, the first thing that comes to their mind is 'Muslim' and you wanted to know whether only Muslims live here. Well, the answer is No, but yeah Muslims are a majority here. If we talk about the whole J & K State, the Muslim population is 70 per cent, Hindus 20 per cent and other religions (Christianity, Jainism, Buddhism, Sikhism, etc.) 10 per cent. All the people here in Kashmir live with a strong brotherhood bond irrespective of their religion. We all believe in an Urdu phrase meaning all the Muslims, Hindus, Sikhs, Christians are brothers. I'll give you an example to prove this. Some two years back, Muslims in the area Shopian helped a poor Hindu to arrange the marriage ceremony of his daughter.

You also talked about the weather and wished that weather in Delhi will be like Kashmir. Trust me you wouldn't want that because, as I mentioned in my last letter, we have really, really cold winter, temperature even drops to -15°C during chil-e-kalan. Weather here is unpredictable as well. Last two days were quite sunny but right now, as I am writing this letter I can hear raindrops outside and the cold is freezing that I can barely hold my pen. The summers here are pleasant, not too warm (for you, for us even 33°C is a very hot day).

I am a good student at school. As I told you before, I am a student of Class IX. I'm preparing for Class IX as well as my matriculation exams. Now the thing that I am struggling with is what subjects to choose after Class X. Do you have any ideas about this? What subjects are you going to choose? According to you, which field has a good scope, good career and requires attention? If you know, please let me know.

Looking forward to your reply.

Your friend,
Duaa

KASHMIR

Saumya had never been to Kashmir. Neither had I. Both of us were embarking on a journey of discovery. There was a sense of anticipation.

But to set the ball rolling, I needed to go to Srinagar. Before Duaa wrote her first letter. Before, it all began.

There were a few reasons. I needed to meet Duaa and her parents. They had asked for it. It was only fair. I was the only link they had, and they wanted to be certain. I would be reassured too, they reasoned. They had asked me to come stay at their home. I didn't take up that offer but agreed to visit.

And, we wanted to film a video with our pen pals, to publish alongside the letters on the BBC's news website. So, the audience could meet the teenagers, put faces to the names and see them in their surroundings, their homes, their hometowns.

Planning a trip to Kashmir is no small task. The constant tension between insurgents and the armed forces means attacks, even suicide attacks, can be commonplace. A seemingly ordinary day can suddenly transform into one with an impassioned crowd, stone pelting or even gunfire. Perception of bias—either towards the state and security forces or the rebels—can invite danger too.

Apart from the threat to physical safety, unannounced curfews can upset well-laid travel plans. Local knowledge of safe exit routes, sensitive areas, accessible health infrastructure was even more crucial in Kashmir. As journalists, the danger didn't deter, but increased our responsibility to ourselves and for the safety of the people we would meet.

Kashmir is categorized as a high-risk area and I had to do a risk assessment exercise for me; my cameraman; the driver we would hire there; and our local contact, a Srinagar-based journalist. It's a detailed brief that the BBC has laid out for travel to any 'hostile environment' around the world. To prepare its journalists in mitigating risk from different kind of threats, like kidnapping, mob violence, attack, etc. We are also issued personal protective equipment, like flak jackets, helmets and a medical kit, to take with us for any eventuality. An editor must decide if the editorial value of covering the story justifies the safety risks being taken by the team.

I couldn't have only gone to Srinagar for just a day. I needed to make our trip count. So, I spent weeks researching other stories we could gather. Slowly, it became an elaborate plan. We now needed to make at least a week-long trip. And travel to rural areas outside the capital city too.

All was not well in Srinagar. The snow had melted, but the cold winds still blew. The city was preparing for a by-election to the parliamentary constituency of Srinagar that had fallen vacant in September 2016, after the member of Parliament resigned, professedly to protest the government's handling of the unrest in the Valley following Burhan Wani's death.[9] More than 1.2 million voters spread across three districts—Ganderbal, Srinagar and Budgam—were to cast their votes on 9 April 2017.[10] Historically, in elections in Jammu and Kashmir, the voter turnout has been lower than the national average—many times, much lower. Reflecting, among other things, a lack of faith in the electoral process.[11]

Polling day turned out to be worse than expected. Srinagar parliamentary constituency recorded the lowest ever turnout. Less than 90,000 voters turned up to cast their vote, as electronic voting machines (EVMs) were destroyed and polling stations came under attack.[12] Eight civilians were killed and 170 injured.[13] A re-poll had to be ordered in many areas, which saw an even lower turnout, just about 2 per cent. That was on 13 April, a day before we were booked on a flight to Srinagar.

That day, there was a crisis in Delhi too. A much more personal one, which I didn't know then would change my life forever. My husband and I had taken the day off to take my father-in-law to our physician. He had been struggling with low-grade fever for a fortnight now and had started looking visibly pale and weak. Yet another round of tests had been done. I had a morning flight to Srinagar the next day and wanted to be around as much as I could before leaving. But the day didn't turn out as planned. Our physician was alarmed with the reports and asked us to immediately take Papa to an oncologist.

An oncologist. A doctor who treats cancer. It took us a moment to understand what he had just suggested. The possibility and definitiveness that came with that diagnosis. We went into autopilot mode. Booking an immediate appointment, taking Papa to the hospital, all the while battling despair. Two hours later, we sat across the desk from a doctor we would come to trust with Papa's life. He gave us a lot of time and patiently explained, in no uncertain words, that Papa didn't have much time left. He had a rare form of cancer that spreads fast and he needed to be admitted to the hospital immediately.

More paperwork, hospital smells, test samples and finally, a bed. We took a breath, huddled around Papa and my husband tried to strike a normal conversation with him. When Papa suddenly said, 'You go home and pack for your Kashmir trip beti, everything is under control, I am in safe hands now. This will take time anyway, and you would be back in a week.'

I smiled. Papa didn't just call me beti, he loved me like I was his daughter. And knew I loved my work passionately. Cancers take time, sometimes years. I didn't know yet, how many Papa had. He was only a few days shy of his sixty-ninth birthday. Would there be any—or many—more? Too much had happened too fast. I looked at my husband. We had already lost his mother five years back. This was not the time to go to work.

I didn't know yet that this would be the best decision of my life. Because Papa wouldn't make it beyond three weeks. Most of which would be spent in hospital, firefighting, getting multiple opinions, clinging to hope.

I stepped out of the hospital. It was already dark. My flight was in twelve hours. I had to start making calls. To my editors, the travel agent, the driver, my cameraman and to the local journalist. I had to make sure that the deployment would happen. I had committed to a work project and everyone had put a lot of effort into it. That had to be respected. A couple of hours later, it was all done. I lay in bed, exhausted. The house had grown very quiet.

The next morning, I called Duaa's parents. They said, they understood. I could hear the disappointment in their voices. But they were kind enough to host Kashif Siddiqui, our cameraperson and Majid Jehangir, a Kashmiri journalist. Over cups of kehwa, hearts were won and trust established. A week or so later, back in our Delhi office, I sat staring at the footage Kashif filmed in Srinagar. And finally, on the screen of a laptop, I met Duaa.

She looked regal as she sat on an expensive carpet in her palatial house, tastefully decorated in shades of brown and maroon. A warm glow reflected on her chubby cheeks. It felt good to see and hear her in her space. In my disoriented state of being, I felt a bit more connected. And curious to see how the girls' different lives would play out in their letters.

Duaa couldn't write in Hindi. Saumya couldn't read Urdu. So Duaa chose English. But Saumya's preferred language was Hindi. She said she could express herself better that way. An agreement was reached. Letters from Srinagar would come in English. The replies from Delhi would be in Hindi. And I would translate for both of them.

It was time to get started. I reached out to both parents and assured them that for the safety of the girls, the letters would not be published in real time but altogether once the exchange was complete. The videos we had filmed would also be released then. And, yes, the letters would be written on paper, but no, they wouldn't be sent by post. Given the disruptions in Kashmir that would have added enormous uncertainty. It was good old email instead. The papers scanned and sent via the internet. A happy marriage of the old and new.

So, finally, we were at the beginning. And like most firsts, it felt tentative. So much depended on the execution of our painstakingly developed idea, which ironically, once set in motion, I had no control over. It would take a life of its own and I would be a bystander as the girls wrote their own stories. An almost physical tension coursed through my already strained shoulders. My life confronting the certainty of a looming end, while it tried to focus on building something new. The joy of getting so far in the project, waxing and waning as my days merged into nights in a seeming free fall. A robotic stubbornness of dealing with one day at a time pulled me along as I waited for Duaa to begin the exchange.

And suddenly, there was that new email in my inbox. The first letter—a simple hello from one teenager to another. Almost an anticlimax after the dramatic build-up. Quite naturally, the first set of letters hovered around introductions. From Duaa's prestigious Presentation Convent School to Saumya's school near her home. From experiencing 7-feet-high snow in 'heaven on Earth' to the sometimes too sunny, too rainy weather of Delhi.

And then Saumya decided to go beyond the obvious. Or rather probe what she knew as the obvious,

I want to know if it's true that only Muslims live there.

Duaa gave her an almost correct make-up of the population of the then state of Jammu and Kashmir (Muslims: 67 per cent, Hindus: 30 per cent, Sikhs: 2 per cent, Buddhists and others: 1 per cent).[14] But that did not tell the unalienable story of religion and Kashmir, underlying Saumya's words,

Whenever the people outside Kashmir hear anything about the Valley, the first thing that comes to their mind is 'Muslim'.

In 1947, when Britain partitioned India into two separate sovereign countries, Lord Mountbatten, the viceroy of India, had set up a Boundaries Commission, and appointed Sir Cyril Radcliffe, a lawyer from London to draw the dividing line. Radcliffe had never been to India before and couldn't distinguish Punjab from Bengal. Perhaps it was this aloofness and distance that made him a suitable candidate in a commission with representatives from both India and Pakistan debating tooth and nail for what they thought was rightfully theirs. The terms of reference were that the demarcation should be on the basis of contiguous Muslim or non-Muslim areas.[15] Broadly, Muslim majority areas were to form Pakistan and non-Muslim majority areas remain in India. But some exceptions were made, sometimes for reasons of geography or existing infrastructure or at other times without offering any explanation. Like in the case of the Muslim-majority city of Gurdaspur, which became part of India. This proved to be controversial not only because it violated the spirit of the terms of reference but also because this gave India the only available land access to Kashmir after Partition.[16]

Jammu and Kashmir, a Muslim-majority state, was ruled at that time by a Hindu, Maharaja Hari Singh. The question he had to consider was whether his kingdom should merge into a country carved to protect the interests of the followers of Islam, Pakistan or, should it accede to the Hindu-majority India, believing that the secular principles that country stands by will protect and uphold the interests of his population too. It was not an easy decision and Maharaja Hari Singh did not want to be rushed. In the months preceding partition, he showed no inclination towards joining Pakistan or staying with India, insisting instead in a meeting with Lord Mountbatten, on Kashmir's independence.[17]

On 15 August 1947, India was partitioned into two sovereign states, but the princely state of Kashmir had not acceded to either. Maharaja Hari Singh wanted to take his time to decide and signed a standstill agreement, which allowed the state to maintain free movement of goods and people across borders with Pakistan too. This, however, changed within a few weeks. In October 1947, the state found itself under attack by Muslim tribesmen from Pakistan. A decision had to be taken. Maharaja Hari Singh asked for Indian army's help to defend his people and signed the instrument of accession with India.

It is around this point that the story varies. Firstly, who supported the Muslim tribesmen's attack? India claims that Pakistan's government and army were behind them while Pakistan alleges that it was a spontaneous act by the Muslim tribesmen to come to the aid of fellow Muslims they perceived to be persecuted by a Hindu king. And secondly, on the sequence of events. India claims that it sent its army to defend Kashmir only after Maharaja Hari Singh asked and agreed to accede.[18] Pakistan disagrees, asserting that the accession happened later, implying that the Maharaja violated the standstill agreement signed with Pakistan by first allowing the Indian army on its soil.[19] What is undisputable is that the instrument of accession retained a clause for holding a plebiscite to find out the will of the people of Jammu and Kashmir when the situation permitted.[20]

The Indian army was able to push the invading tribesmen back, but only up to a point. Pakistan gained control of a part of northern Kashmir, referred to as Azad Kashmir (Free Kashmir) or Pakistan-administered Kashmir, depending on which side of the boundary (now, Line of Control, or LoC) you stood. More than seventy years, a few wars and an armed insurgency later, Kashmir remains a bone of contention between India and Pakistan. And the plebiscite remains an unfulfilled promise to the people of Kashmir.

Kashmir—the name that has been loosely used to refer to the whole of the former state of Jammu and Kashmir. When protestors have raised slogans like: '*Kashmir hamara hai*' (Kashmir is ours). When Bollywood has made films like *Mission Kashmir*. When Saumya comments:

> *Whenever the people outside Kashmir hear anything about the Valley, the first thing that comes to their mind is 'Muslim'*

The map of the region, now divided into two union territories, gives some context. Kashmir division occupies less than 16 per cent of the former state's geographical area, Jammu about 26 per cent and Ladakh, 58 per cent.[21] But Kashmir houses more than half the area's population (54 per cent) while Jammu has 44 per cent and Ladakh, only a little over 2 per cent.[22] Now add to this mix of numbers, the religious composition of the three divisions. The population in Kashmir is overwhelmingly Muslim (97 per cent). In Jammu, Hindus (65 per cent) are in majority. And Ladakh has an almost even number of Muslims (47 per cent) and Buddhists (46 per cent).[23] Views across these regions have been divergent. An opinion poll conducted by the Centre for the Study of Developing Societies in 2007 found that nearly 90 per cent of people surveyed in Srinagar favoured independence for Kashmir while 95 per cent respondents in Jammu city wanted the state to be a part of India.[24]

This had started becoming clear very early on. After Kashmir's accession to India, with the help of then Indian Prime Minister Jawaharlal Nehru, effective power in the state was transferred from Maharaja Hari Singh to the Jammu and Kashmir Prime Minister Sheikh Abdullah,[25] a towering Muslim leader who espoused secular ideals. In that endeavour, he even changed the name of his political party from All Jammu and Kashmir Muslim Conference to Jammu and Kashmir National Conference in 1939. At the time of the attack by Pakistani tribesmen, his party formed volunteer forces and assisted Indian soldiers when the government found itself caught unawares.[26]

Sheikh Abdullah was revered in the Valley and claimed to enjoy popular support across the State. But some of Jammu's Hindus felt that their desire to merge into India was not understood by him and inspired by the Hindu nationalist organization Rashtriya Swayamsevak Sangh (RSS)[27], formed a Praja Parishad (People's Party) to voice it. Whilst Sheikh Abdullah negotiated preconditions with the Indian government to enable Kashmir retain some autonomy through a special status under Article 370, Praja Parishad demanded complete integration into the country. It led many protest marches against the then-agreed terms of joining India, especially, retaining the designation of the head of the state government as prime minister and keeping the state flag.[28] The movement enjoyed overwhelming support of the Hindus of Jammu at that time. And while its electoral performance waxed and waned over the decades, the interests it represented, endured, as more recent elections victories would testify. The members of Praja Parishad in Kashmir would eventually become part of the present-day Bharatiya Janata Party (BJP).[29]

This diversity and divisions within the region are sometimes not widely understood outside it. Nor are the complexities and competing interests they bring in. The Kashmiri identity looms large. And within that, the exodus of the Kashmiri Hindu community (also known as Kashmiri Pandits) is often forgotten, shrouded in a cloak of silence.

With the rise of militancy in the Kashmir Valley in 1989–90, hundreds of thousands of Kashmiri Pandits were terrorized into leaving. Most were never able to return. It strained the religious harmony in the region for decades to come. But that's a question Saumya would ask much later. And till then, all she had was Duaa's experience of an enduring brotherhood. Which Duaa insisted on by giving evidence:

I'll give you an example to prove this. Some two years back, Muslims in the area Shopian helped a poor Hindu to arrange the marriage ceremony of his daughter.

Duaa. The next generation. Born in the new millennium. Writing from her experience of love.

Delhi
14 May 2017

Dear Duaa,

I got your letter. How are you? How is Aveen?

It is summer holidays in Delhi right now and I have just returned after spending ten days in Bihar's Madhubani where my cousin was getting married. It was neither too hot nor cold in Bihar. The biggest problem there was power cuts. Even then, I enjoyed spending some days away from the hectic life in Delhi. Do you also have a family home in a village and have you ever had a chance to go there? I'd like to know how you feel when you visit your village.

You had asked my opinion about choosing subjects for tenth standard. In Delhi, subjects are chosen after completing tenth standard and I want to study science. You can take whichever subject you like, but according to me, science opens up more options. According to me, one should choose the subject one is interested in.

These days, Kashmir is in the news especially because of 'stone pelting girls'. Can you tell me more about this, why are girls doing that? Are they really being harassed or troubled?

Also, often we hear that schools and colleges are shut and internet services also closed down. When schools-colleges are shut, how is the course completed? And when internet services are shut down, then how do you remain in touch with your friends and remain active on social media?

an act of defence. What would you have done if you were in that situation? Please answer that question. I want to know.

You also asked about the shutting down of schools-colleges and snapping of internet services. When the schools are shut, we the students have to complete the whole course ourselves and if the shutting of schools coincides with the snapping of internet services—it is a headache. Can you imagine being confined to the four walls of your home with no internet, no social media like WhatsApp, Instagram, etc? Because of the snapping, we can't remain active on social media. Right now, all the social media is banned, but people can still access the banned sites through VPN. We cannot remain in touch with our friends. We can only talk to them over phone or sometimes not even that because calling facilities are also snapped. We live in the era of internet, the twenty-first century, but sometimes I feel that I am living in the seventeenth century. The snapping of these basic services always gets on my nerves because every human has the right to information and by snapping the internet I feel we are being deprived of that right.

Well, I really want to know what life in Delhi is like? Is it boring, hectic or fun?

Looking forward to your reply.

Until next time.

Your friend,
Duaa

PS: I study in Presentation Convent School, which is a girls' higher secondary school here, so I don't get to interact with boys that much. It's not like girls and boys live separately. There are many co-educational institutions in the Valley, like my school was four decades ago. After that, it became a girls' school and another school, our sister school—Burn Hall—formed the boys' school.

BATTLES

For any young girl in Kashmir, 2017 was a difficult summer to write dispassionately, to answer questions about stone pelting and internet shutdowns. Still, Duaa tried.

It was a year on from the summer when rebel icon Burhan Wani was killed. And it wasn't the first summer when youth used stones against security forces' pellet guns. Yet, the stakes seemed higher and the fight closer than ever before.

Even if one wanted to walk away, social media brought it close. The raw as-it-happens glimpse of the unreported made it a powerful medium. This was the very reason that led to internet shutdowns. Social media took away the formal telling of news, made citizens the journalists and democratized access to information. But the information, when it managed to trickle into smartphones and computers, was troubling and bared the ever-deepening fissures.

As it did in April 2017, the day before my planned trip to Srinagar. After reports of a historically low turnout (7 per cent) in the Srinagar parliamentary constituency by-elections, which separatists had called to boycott, and the death of eight civilians in the ensuing violent clashes, had been played out in newspapers and TV channels.

A couple of days later, other videos started surfacing, which were filmed on phones by non-journalists (verified by the BBC as genuine) and shared on WhatsApp. The first one captured a group of young men heckling some Central Reserve Police Force (CRPF) men as they carried EVMs from a polling booth.[30] One man kicked a CRPF jawan, hit him on the head, causing his helmet to roll down on the road. Other men crowded around the group of CRPF men, filming them shouting 'Go India, go back!' and '*Hai haq yeh hamara, Azadi, hum lekar rahenge, Azadi*' (Freedom is our right, we won't rest till we get our freedom). The jawan continued to walk. Neither he nor his armed peers stopped to engage or argue with the young men.

Their restraint in the face of provocation got lauded as the video was splashed on TV screens across the country. In the Valley, where faith in political parties and the government was at an all-time low, this confrontation exposed the challenges in executing the democratic process of elections. For the jawans, it was a challenging task—to help conduct free and fair polling in the midst of a people who consider the whole act a sham. And be seen as the face of an oppressive system, opening them up to the rage of civilians. It all boiled down to what they did in that situation. In that video, their control and calm, in place of attack and anger, was on display. A message that travelled far and wide. But that was far from the only reality of the Valley's experience with security forces.

A few days later, my phone beeped again. This time it was a Twitter alert. A tweet with a video we had been replaying and sharing among journalists in a bid to confirm its veracity. It showed a man tied to the bonnet of an army jeep with a paper stuck to his chest. The jeep was followed by an army mine-protected vehicle and a warning could be heard as they drove past, 'This is the fate that will befall stone pelters'. The same warning was written on the paper.

Even without knowing the context, the sight of an unarmed man, sitting atop a tyre, with his arms and body tied to an army vehicle, sent shivers down the spine. Because it indicated an extremely fraught situation, and one felt for his extreme vulnerability.

The video had been tweeted by a former chief minister of the state.[31] It turned out that the video was filmed on 9 April, the day of the election. Later, in a press conference, an army officer Major Leetul Gogoi recounted that he was called to rescue election commission officials stuck inside a polling booth in Budgam, about 30 km from Srinagar, as it had been surrounded by stone pelters protesting the election. He claimed that to resolve the situation without injury to civilians and the armed forces, he saw it fit to use a protestor as a 'human shield'.[32]

The image of Farooq Ahmad Dar tied to that army jeep caused an uproar for being a grave human rights violation, and the Indian government ordered an inquiry into the incident. Even before that was completed, Major Gogoi was commended by the Indian army for his 'sustained efforts over a period of time'. The Indian army chief, General Bipin Rawat said that 'You fight a dirty war with innovations'.[33]

For Farooq Ahmad Dar, this day changed his life. The image of being tied to the army jeep preceded him wherever he went, as did his defence. And he claimed he was ostracized for it. There were two reasons.

Farooq Ahmad Dar vehemently denied Major Gogoi's allegation that he participated in stone pelting that day. This did not make him a popular man. He claimed he had cast his vote that day and was driving elsewhere on his bike when he was caught in the crossfire. This faith in the democratic process also didn't find him public favour.

That was Farooq Ahmad Dar's paradox. The army called him a stone-pelter and his village boycotted him for being a government agent. It just made one thing clear to him. In multiple interviews, he said, he'd made a mistake that he would never repeat again.[34] In the next parliamentary elections in 2019, Farooq Ahmad Dar was put on elections duty. But his family told journalists,[35] he did not vote.[36]

Despite the princely state of Kashmir acceding to India in 1947, a separatist sentiment persisted in the Valley. For different people it meant different things. It could be opposition to accession by India and integration with the Islamic Republic of Pakistan for some, or a desire for self-rule for others. The armed rebellion that strengthened and gained popular support in 1989–90 was one expression of that.

In 1993, the separatist sentiment found a clear political voice when the All Parties Hurriyat Conference (APHC) was founded. This was an amalgamation of more than two dozen religious and political groups that wanted independence for Kashmir by peaceful means, though most of the groups had their armed wings too.[37] Many of their leaders spoke about intimidation, harassment and violence at the hands of Indian security forces as a reason for losing faith in democratic processes and joining the movement. APHC brought together disparate ideologies united by their single aim and slowly, they started being seen as a force to reckon with, as representatives of the people. Their support, sought after by both India and Pakistan, often in times of unrest and negotiation.[38]

Over the years, the group broke into different splinters headed by prominent separatist leaders—Syed Ali Shah Geelani, Mirwaiz Umar Farooq and Yasin Malik,[39] among others—each representing a peaceful but different path to Kashmir's final goal of self-rule. One similarity endured— that they would not participate in the Indian electoral process at any level. Their calls to boycott elections would mostly be widely adhered to. They would organize strikes and shutdowns. Mobilize a sentiment that encouraged stone pelting.

At fifteen, Duaa was too young to vote. But she was old enough to observe and consider the battles around her: online and offline. On the streets. Outside schools. Among those of her age. Young students carrying on with their daily lives. Sheltered safely inside the walls of their schools. Exposed to the presence of armed security personnel stationed outside on street corners. A tense coexistence broken quite regularly by stones.

For most of her growing-up years, Duaa had seen and heard of stone pelting. An act of rebellion. A symbol of defiance. Mostly fronted by boys and young men. Sometimes spontaneous. Many times, organized in response to calls by separatist leaders.[40] To show a lack of faith in governments and renew their demand for 'freedom'.[41]

The act of pelting stones wasn't alien to Kashmir, but it seemed that the Valley fully embraced it in the summer of 2008 when protests broke out after the government passed an order to transfer nearly 100 acres of forest land to the Amarnath shrine board, which manages the annual Hindu pilgrimage, the Amarnath Yatra. The order triggered the apprehension that this was the beginning of a plan to change the demographic of the Muslim-majority state. Thousands spilled on to the streets in protest in some of biggest pro-independence demonstrations seen in the Valley after the 1990s. Calls of 'Azadi' rang loud and clear.[42] As the government pushed back, putting restrictions and curfew in place, the '*kan-i-jung*', or stone pelting, became the war cry. Young men confronting armed security forces with stones. Attack and retreat. As the forces fired to bring back order, at least sixty people died. The government buckled, taking back its order, but that led to protests in Hindu-dominated Jammu. An eventual blockade of the Srinagar-Jammu national highway, the only functional link connecting Kashmir Valley with India. The clashes went on for two months during which more than 1000 people were injured.[43]

For years before that, stone pelting was a weekly ritual that took place near Srinagar's Jama Masjid after Friday prayers. Shops would down their shutters, and streets empty out as young men would target a police post with stones. But now it became a form of political protest. The state police claimed that these protestors were not politically motivated, but unemployed youth addicted to drugs and earning a quick buck by agreeing to pelt stones for as little as Rs 100 to Rs 300. Some academics argued that these young men were being sentimentally swayed for political gains by separatist leaders who wanted to bolster their power by encouraging these street protests.[44]

The young men disagree. One stone pelter, when asked for his reasons, said, 'I read and I understand. That's why I pelt stones. I would love to join peaceful protests. But they don't let us gather, not even for shouting slogans and expressing our anger.' He blames the government's pushback on protests in 2008 for his 'baptism' into stone pelting.[45]

Others clearly speak of stones as an expression to voice their desire for 'freedom'. In 2008, nearly 1,800 security personnel were injured in those protests and around 400 vehicles damaged. More than 600 young men were charged with stone pelting. These charges were withdrawn in 2016 when Mehbooba Mufti announced an amnesty for stone pelters.[46] An administrative act that would be used repeatedly over the years as stone pelting became a mainstay of protests in the Valley.

This summer, it wasn't just the boys. Media was flooded with striking images of young girls in white uniforms. School bag on shoulders, a football in arm and a stone in hand.[47] It wasn't that young women had not participated in the stone pelting protests over the previous years. During the 2008 Amarnath land controversy, girls had started protesting inside college campuses. In 2009, following the Shopian rape and murder case and in 2010 when a tear gas shell by security forces killed Tufail Mattoo, women protested and pelted stones. Many times, facing jibes by fellow male protestors.[48] Women's fight for equal rights has always transcended borders, pushed boundaries.

In this particular incident, referred to in Duaa's letter, it was a twenty-one-year-old football coach, Afshan Ashiq. She claimed to have been leading some female students to practise when they came across policemen who were controlling another protest. She says their 'high-handedness' and abusive language towards girls provoked her into instinctively defending her young team members.[49] Once she picked up stones, her students followed suit. Later in an interview, Afshan explained her reasons. She spoke of standing up to injustice, but criticized Kashmiri separatists for inspiring stone pelting as much as she censured the security personnel who she said had provoked her. Despite her 'spontaneous' month. The three-page government order cited maintenance of public order as the justification.

This order was announced right after Duaa wrote her first letter. I didn't really have to insist that she don't look up Saumya on social media—she couldn't anyway. For most part of their letter exchange, the ban remained in place. It riled her up, as it would any teenager, born into an age where access to internet and social media is taken for granted. It made Saumya realize her privilege. Among the many other battles Duaa had, this too was one that Saumya did not have to witness or fight.

Delhi
27 May 2017

Dear Duaa,

I am fine here and my family is also doing well. Right now, my father's sister has come to spend holidays at our home. Samarth is also fine, but his pranks haven't reduced at all. I hope you and your family are well too.

After reading your last letter, it became clear that our society is not safe for girls, whether it is in Delhi, Kashmir or any other place. Girls in Delhi do keep some things with them for self-defence, but even then they are harassed. Like recently in Haryana, a 'Nirbhaya' type incident was repeated with another girl. In that sense, no Indian city is safe. But after reading your story about the 'stone pelting girls', I couldn't understand one thing—why did the army attack those girls? Army is for our safety, right? I'd like to tell you that if I would get stuck in such a situation, I would have reacted in a similar way to protect myself.

You had asked me about life in Delhi. Life is 'mast' here. Ramazan is about to begin here and it is very festive in Old Delhi area these days. There are lots of people around India Gate too and it remains lively even around midnight. One can't even imagine life without internet or other means of communication in Delhi. I feel very bad that people in Kashmir have to live through such difficult circumstances.

I have a question for you—would you like to live in any other Indian city for your higher studies? And can any student from Kashmir live comfortably and happily in any other city in the country?

I feel sad that students in Kashmir have to live without internet and social media sometimes. But are only some miscreants responsible for this situation or is there some other reason? If it inconveniences people there so much, then why is internet and social media shut down there?

I had read about a sixteen-year-old boy who had made a social media app called 'Kash-book' in the news. Do you also use it or does anyone you know use it?

Tell me, aren't Kashmiri people tired of this situation?

Waiting for your reply.

Your friend,
Saumya

Srinagar
29 May 2017

Dear Saumya,

It's good to know that you and your family are fine and doing well. Me and my family are doing well as well. From the way you describe Samarth, he is just as mischievous as Aveen. Last week we had a school picnic to Sonmarg. 'Son' as in 'sona' (gold) in Kashmiri and 'marg' is 'valley', so Sonmarg literally means 'the valley of gold'. It is called so because it is situated in a higher region from which you can see various mountaintops covered in snow (throughout the year) and when the sunrays strike the snow in the morning, it seems like gold. I wanted to know where do you go for your school picnic?

In your letter you asked me various questions. About the army. Let me first clear that it wasn't the army but the security personnel and police. There is a difference. It is a mystery why they attacked the girls in the first place. Nobody knows, nobody but them. As for your other question, I wouldn't like to be in any other Indian city. For my higher studies, I have planned that I will either stay in Kashmir or go out abroad because honestly I am frightened to be in any other Indian city as a student. There has been news and I am sure you must have heard them, that many Kashmiri students, including girls, being victim of various types of ragging in reputed universities and students thrown out of the college in the dead of the night just for being Kashmiris. You must know that Kashmiris are known for their 'Kashmiriyat', meaning our hospitality, our simplicity and our kind and honest hearts. If you go outside the country to any country and tell the locals that you are a Kashmiri, they will treat you like a family member or like an old friend because they know how we treat our guests. I know it sounds very boring, but you will not understand it unless you experience it yourself. So I invite you and your family to be my guests and explore Kashmir.

You told me about a sixteen-year-old who has made an app, 'Kash-book'. I haven't used it as yet nor do I know anyone who uses it. But this example is a proof that we people have tremendous talent. All we need is a platform to showcase our talents. But unfortunately, the officials in charge don't understand. We people could be on top of the world but without proper platforms only few are able to make it to the top spot.

As for the internet ban, only government can answer why they are imposing ban on internet and taking the right to information away from us. Honestly, people have become habitual to these scenarios. We have been experiencing these situations since the time of our forefathers.

Waiting for your next letter really badly.

Your friend,
Duaa

PS: I have attached some pictures of Sonmarg just so that you can see for yourself how beautiful it is.

PERCEPTIONS

Saumya's questions were innocent and honest. She wanted to understand.

> *I couldn't understand one thing—why did the army attack those girls? Army is for our safety, right?*

The Indian armed forces are a hallowed institution. They represent an idea beyond the individual. For the greater common good. Men and women, who choose to train to be physically and mentally tough enough to fight, kill or even die. Sacrifice their life for the nation. To defend its borders, its people.

Saumya had grown up watching an elaborate parade on 26 January, India's Republic Day, every year. It was a winter morning ritual common across millions of homes in the country. Over rounds of tea and breakfast they watched the more than three-hour-long live broadcast that went through the same motions every year but never tired its viewers. In fact, the routine built a bond. When the President would unfurl the national flag, stand in salute, the national anthem would be played, and Saumya would leave her favourite spot on the sofa in front of the television in her house and jump into attention too, singing along till the end. A moment of patriotic fervour.

As columns upon columns of soldiers would march on, her chest swelled up in pride. And eyes welled up when she heard the battle accounts of the bravehearts being honoured with the likes of Shaurya (courage), Vir (brave), Kirti (glory) Chakras, the titles underscoring their heroism. Sometimes these were accepted posthumously by their wives, sisters, mothers. Who stood stoically, as they awaited their turn, fighting a million memories tearing their heavy heart.

Every year, that day, the Indian prime minister would lay a wreath at the '*Amar Jawan Jyoti*' (eternal flame), a memorial built in 1972 to commemorate the soldiers who died fighting the 1971 war against Pakistan. Tourists from around the country and the world posed for pictures against the inverted bayonet with a soldier's helmet over it as they visited the iconic India Gate in Delhi, the war memorial to remember soldiers in the British Indian army who died fighting in World War I.

The army fighting the 'external' foreign enemy to defend its own people, its country's sovereignty. Popular cinema too, built on that perception. War films, like *Border* (1997), based on the 1971 India-Pakistan war and *Haqeeqat* (Reality, 1964), based on the 1962 Indo-China war that immortalized the Indian army's sacrifices were broadcast on TV channels around Republic Day and Independence Day every year. Their songs—'Sandese aate hain' (Messages come for us) and 'Kar chale hum fida' (We have decided to dedicate) that portrayed the human side of the soldier, his pain, solitude, possible martyrdom and 'Ae mere watan ke logon' (O people of my country), hailing his bravado—remained hummable and deeply felt. Saumya once said that patriotic songs like 'Ae mere watan ke logon' gave her goosebumps and made her cry.

There was another factor that influenced Saumya's relationship with the Indian army. Her parents used to work at a petrol pump, whose owner was a war widow. Her husband had been martyred during the Kargil stand-off in Kashmir in 1999, when India and Pakistan came head-to-head in a warlike situation. On 26 July 1999, the Indian army successfully recaptured all the posts that had been occupied by Pakistan's army. Since then that day was marked every year as Kargil Diwas (Kargil Day) to remember Indian soldiers' sacrifices. Saumya grew up witnessing the annual commemoration on Kargil Diwas and said it instilled a sense of pride in her young mind. She felt attached to the Indian army. Knowing the family of an army man made their sacrifices for the country feel very close and real.

Saumya's references clashed with the picture that Duaa's letter evoked. And it wasn't just the letter, as she engaged more with Kashmir, she could not escape the reports of pellet gun injuries, pictures of bloodied protestors of her own age that filled the newspapers and TV bulletins those nights, telling the story of the fight with the 'internal' challenge.[56] When the army was engaging with its country's own citizens and not an external enemy across the border.

Duaa had clarified in her letter that in the particular clash with the girls' football coach that Saumya referred to, it was the police and not the army that was involved. The state police is a force made up of locals while the army is made up of soldiers from all over the country. And the army has been deeply involved in Kashmir. Not just in defending the borders from office after rumours emerged that he was making efforts for Kashmir's independence. One source of these rumours was when Abdullah met with an American politician, and it was speculated that they discussed possible financial aid that US would be willing to commit to in the event of Kashmir's independence.[61] Abdullah was put under arrest by the *Sadr-i-Riyasat* (head of state) Karan Singh on charges of anti-national activity. Nehru did not challenge the dismissal or arrest. This saw the emergence of a new party, Plebiscite Front, formed by one of the senior leaders of National Conference.[62] The party campaigned for a United Nations-monitored plebiscite to ascertain the will of the Kashmiri people. Many of its leaders were imprisoned or banished.

In 1962, India lost a war with China and Nehru's health took a downturn. Despite not opposing Sheikh Abdullah's arrest, Nehru still believed that he was the only leader with the stature to renew negotiations on Kashmir's status. Abdullah was released in 1964 to give him a chance at reaching a resolution. Upon his release, Abdullah's speeches made it clear that he no longer had the same pro-India stance he had held at the time of independence. He spoke of greater autonomy and the will of Kashmiri people as he addressed rallies of Plebiscite Front supporters. He spoke of his state as 'a bride cherished by two husbands'—India and Pakistan—'neither of whom cared to ascertain what the Kashmiris wanted'. He even addressed a rally in Rawalpindi in Pakistan, met then president of Pakistan, Ayub Khan, and was on his way to Muzaffarabad when news of Nehru's sudden death reached him.[63] The negotiations had to be halted and Sheikh Abdullah was rearrested in 1965.

The year 1971 saw the creation of Bangladesh after India defeated Pakistan in a war and firmly established its military superiority. The Plebiscite Front was barred from contesting elections. Sheikh Abdullah, who had been released, started coming to terms with letting go of the demand for a plebiscite for Kashmir. The Plebiscite Front was wound up and the National Conference revived. Then prime minister Indira Gandhi even negotiated an accord with him.

In 1975, Sheikh Abdullah was sworn in as the head of the Congress Parliamentary Party in the Kashmir state assembly and returned as chief minister. The Kashmir Accord gave up the demand of a plebiscite, in lieu of the people being given the right to self-determination by a democratically elected government as envisaged under Article 370, rather than the governments that had ruled the state till then.[64] Signing the Accord was an unpopular decision in the Valley and the relationship between Abdullah and Gandhi deteriorated.

The year 1977 became an important milestone for both India and Kashmir. This was the year when the Congress party lost power in the Central government for the first time in independent India. Janata Party, an alliance of Opposition parties formed to protest the hugely repressive Emergency imposed by Indira Gandhi, won a majority and formed the government.

A few months later, elections were held in Jammu and Kashmir. The National Conference fought these elections on its own. This gave the semblance of a credible opposition in the state. Three decades after the country's independence, the elections in Jammu and Kashmir were for the first time considered to be free and fair.

By this time, Praja Parishad had first merged into Bharatiya Jana Sangh, then into Janata Party (breaking away in 1980 to form BJP).[65] The National Conference won a comfortable majority, but most of its wins were in the Kashmir Valley. The seats in Jammu evenly split between Congress and Janata Party.[66] Sheikh Abdullah was sworn in as chief minister and was succeeded by his son, Farooq Abdullah after his death in 1982.

But by 1987, the National Conference and Congress were again fighting together in the state assembly elections. The newly formed Muslim United Front (MUF), a group of Islamic Kashmiri political parties including the Jamaat-e-Islami (a religious party formed in 1941 in Lahore, undivided India)[67] stood in opposition. It represented a sentiment that combined religion with political assertion, a view that had always existed in the Valley but had not been actively represented in the political mainstream.

The elections were widely reported to be rigged with MUF candidates winning only four seats and losing many by very few votes.[68] The pro-Pakistan and pro-independence aspirations that were captured by the Plebiscite Front in the 1960–70s were ripe for being inflamed again. Many MUF leaders were imprisoned. There was a widespread perception of disillusionment with the promise of democracy in India, a tipping point that encouraged a pro-Pakistan sentiment in the Valley.[69]

Pakistan saw this as an opportunity to renew its efforts at claiming Kashmir. The country's Inter-Services Intelligence (ISI) had been working in a clandestine operation to provide foreign aid and refuge to Afghan militia fighting a Soviet invasion of Afghanistan. For almost a decade, this funding was used to establish hundreds of madrasas (religious schools) in Pakistan's cities and frontier areas. When the Soviets left Afghanistan in 1989, the fighters and equipment developed with western aid became Pakistan's property,[70] ready to be used when political disquiet started bubbling over in Kashmir.

Many of the MUF leaders are believed to have fled to Pakistan in 1989 to take training in arms and return to the Valley to lead a militant struggle. The ISI ran camps for them and the young men they inspired (a charge Pakistan denies), also enabling free movement across the border from Kashmir. The JKLF,[71] which was formed as an offshoot of the Plebiscite Front in the 1960s and operated largely from London and Pakistan-administered Kashmir, found a new life across the border in India now. Young men who had campaigned for leaders of the MUF in the 1987 elections and felt cheated by the democratic process, were motivated to become JKLF cadres.[72] Suicide attacks targeting symbols of state became a widely used tool, indicating the level of indoctrination and frustration.

Though it began as an assertion for self-rule, this movement soon acquired a religious fervour. Instead of the JKLF, which was secular and pro-independence, Pakistan encouraged the newly emerging militant arm of the Jamaat-e-Islami, the Hizbul Mujahideen that favoured merger with the Islamic state of Pakistan.[73] Under their influence and pressure, cinema halls were closed, drinking and smoking banned and women asked to cover themselves in burqa. Despite this, they had popular support. Militants freely mingled with people who often gave them refuge.

In January 1990, chief minister Farooq Abdullah resigned. There was virtually no state machinery working any more. The armed forces sent in to protect the people, started being viewed as an occupying force. They had the unenviable task of safeguarding a people who did not want that security, who felt misunderstood and were instead bound to protect those they felt truly represented their aspirations. Faced with suicide attacks and bomb blasts by militants at an alarming regularity, security forces conducted massive search operations that could be brutal towards civilians unwilling to give up information on the insurgents.[74] The clashes destroyed houses and localities. Thousands were injured or disabled for life, many were disappeared, businesses and lives collapsed. The Valley lost all resemblance to its previous life.

Deaths were daily and countless. Various authors and reports attribute conflicting numbers caused by the armed forces and by militants. Deaths occurred in the crossfire between militants and army, when processions or demonstrations were fired upon, and many times, persons would just disappear from the custody of armed forces. Given the support to militants among locals, the security forces were often accused of turning their anger on them as reprisal for militant attacks. Some estimates suggest that 20,000 people had died by the end of 1995.[75]

The armed forces were given additional powers. Special laws in force in Jammu and Kashmir—the Jammu and Kashmir Public Safety Act (PSA, 1978), the Terrorist and Disruptive Activities (Prevention) Act (TADA, 1987)[76] and the Armed Forces (Jammu and Kashmir) Special Powers Act (AFSPA, 1990)—were used against thousands of people. They provided the security forces with sweeping powers of arrest and detention, with powers to shoot to kill and with immunity from prosecution.

There was widespread reporting of their misuse and criticism that they lacked vital legal safeguards. Human rights groups—including Amnesty International, Human Rights Watch, People's Union for Civil Liberties, the Coordination Committee on Kashmir and the Committee for Initiative on Kashmir—detailed horrific accounts of custodial torture, resulting in lifelong disability and death. Most of the victims were young men, detained during 'crackdown' or 'cordon and search' operations to identify militants.[77] This tactic has been recounted in detail by many, including Kashmiri journalist Basharat Peer in his book *Curfewed Night.*[78] These operations involved isolating an area, getting all the men out of their houses so the security forces could search their houses for sheltering any militants. The men could also be paraded in front of an informer who would indicate if he suspected them to be sympathizers or rebels and if identified so, they would be taken away.

And then there were women, the often unreported casualty of conflicts. Various studies recorded accounts of widespread fear among women.[79] The armed conflict impacted their daily lives, not only with violence and sexual harassment but also anxiety about it. It restricted their movement. Many dropped out of schools and colleges for fear of violence on the streets. Families started marrying off their women at a young age for their 'safety', sometimes even by force. But this was no solution, as a high incidence of domestic violence underscored. Many agreed that they felt more vulnerable, and women's participation and representation in political movements was adversely affected. Their roles reduced to 'victims'—of rape, kidnapping, molestation.

There were reports of sexual assaults and mass rapes at the hands of the armed forces.[80] The most infamous one perhaps was allegedly committed in 1991 in the far-flung twin villages of Kunan and Poshpora. The women of those villages allege that late on an icy cold February night, the army conducted a 'cordon and search' operation and gang-raped a large number of women and tortured the men. The army has always denied these allegations. In a response for a BBC report following up on the case, an army spokesperson said, 'These allegations had been independently investigated three times, and that the case had been closed due to conflicting statements.'[81]

The case was in the public eye in the first place only because the women survivors insisted on filing a First Information Report (FIR) with the police.[82] This was an act of considerable bravery in the 1990s, when—as now—there was a lot of stigma associated with rape. A raped woman was considered 'defiled' and many times not accepted back into her family.

Many such alleged atrocities were reported at that time. But the majority were never formally reported to the police and judicial system, only shared with journalists or activists. In their reports and articles, they underscored that the immunity granted to troops from prosecution and court martial proceedings acted as a deterrent to filing complaints.[83]

Findings from a study on violence and its impact on health done by Médecins Sans Frontières in 2005 suggested the wide scale of abuse. 'Sexual violence is a common strategy used to terrorize and intimidate people in conflict, but in Kashmir it is an issue that is not openly discussed. Nevertheless, 11.6 per cent of interviewees said they had been victims of sexual violence since 1989. Almost two-thirds of the people interviewed (63.9 per cent) had heard over a similar period about cases of rape, while one in seven had witnessed rape.'[84] The figures are much higher than that of Sierra Leone, Sri Lanka and Chechnya.

After the initial investigation, the Kunan-Poshpora rape case got mired in the system. Till more than two decades later in 2013, when a group of fifty young women decided to renew the legal battle. The case is still in court, but the involvement of a new generation of women completely disconnected from the survivors, yet willing to take up the issue of sexual violence and alleged immunity, speaks volumes of their empowerment, sisterhood and a quest for justice.

Five of these petitioners have authored a book. One of them, Essar Batool, recounts her impressions about the army while growing up in the early 2000s, before she says she began to 'read and understand' and eventually decided to pursue the Kunan-Poshpora case. 'For a long time, I was of the view that people exaggerated when they spoke of the excesses of the Indian armed forces; they weren't so bad, these army men who were present in almost every corner of my city. Weren't they protecting us?'[85]

History gives perspective. For generations like those of Duaa—born after the insurgent 1990s, after militancy had been brought under control, after daily violence had ebbed, but while the presence of the forces persists, and a new rebellion rears its head at the horizon stirring alive latent fears—it brings a conundrum: should one inform one's life and opinions by what they are witnessing in the present or by what has been recorded in words, songs and memories of the past? To look ahead to the future or look back at the history.

And in Kashmir, it is still not easy to reveal where you are looking. Feigned ignorance or a refusal to take a strong position is often a safe place. Not denying the past or one's personal experience of it, but refusing to publicly acknowledge its lasting influence.

To enable dreaming of a safe future. It's a silent and difficult choice.

Delhi
1 June 2017

Dear Duaa,

How are you? And how is your family?

In your previous letter, you had asked me about where my school takes us for picnics. This year our school took us to Manesar, a rural area outside Delhi. We stayed at a resort in Manesar. We were driven around in a tractor there and got familiar with village life.

I saw the photos of Sonmarg that you sent. And after seeing them, I feel like coming to Kashmir.

When I had asked you in my previous letter about whether you'd like to study in any city of India, I was not surprised by your answer. That is because I am also familiar with the treatment meted to Kashmiris. I wish our society was able to save children from this kind of behaviour.

The kind of inhuman behaviour spreading in our society is not restricted to Kashmiris but towards people of any different region. Ragging is also an expression of that.

When I read about a man being used as 'human shield' in the newspaper, it made me very sad. Such incidents only encourage more inhuman activities.

Sometimes I wonder, can't we end this inhumanity from human society? And that there are no restrictions to go or come from any part of the world.

Sometimes I get to know from newspapers that Kashmiris want freedom. I want to know whom do they want freedom from? And why has Kashmir still not seen development?

From your letter, I also got to know that schools shut down in Kashmir for six-seven months. So, I feel that children would find it difficult to pass time and the kind of fear pervading all the time, it must make it very hard for them to develop fully. I'd like to know what you think about this. Are you not tired of this state of affairs?

In the end, I'd like to close my letter with some hope, that a time will come when anyone will be able to go anywhere and it won't bother anyone. Everyone will live with each other with a lot of love.

Waiting for your next letter.

Your friend,
Saumya

Srinagar
5 June 2017

Dear Saumya,

Received your letter and I'm glad to know that you liked Sonmarg. If you want to come here, you are very much welcome to be my guest.

I am informed that this is my last letter to you for the project, but I'd definitely like to be in touch with you. I saw our video and the first letter on BBC Hindi and Urdu website today and I must say this, that I am totally spellbound right now. The reaction of my friends and family was awesome. They loved the video and the letter. I hope it was the same with your family and friends as well.

In your letter you asked me what Kashmiris want freedom from. We want freedom from cruelty of the world, freedom from discrimination, freedom from the people who think that we are inferior to them. Trust me we are not inferiors but equals. I know it must sound quite confusing, but if you want to understand what Kashmiris want freedom from then, I highly recommend you watch the Bollywood movie *Haider*. Everything in that movie about Kashmir is true. Everything but the English accent of the people. We don't pronounce planted as 'pllaantted' or hurted as 'huurrttted'. Regarding the development part, you must know that Kashmir was one of the first states in India to start development. We had India's second hydropower project, the concept of development of proper school, girl child education, western hospitals, etc., were all here in around 1900s, i.e. before independence, before the rest of India. These developments took place under the Dogra rule in J & K. Even my school (which is a missionary school) was built during the reign of Maharaja Hari Singh. So you see, Kashmir could have been the most developed state of India, but over time the governing bodies and administration became corrupt and also the situation didn't allow us to go for development. But it's not like we are not developing, we are also developing like the rest of India. You asked me whether people were tired of the state of affairs. As I mentioned in my previous letter that we've become habitual of the situation here and if a person is habitual to a situation, he does not feel tired.

I'm closing my last letter with a hope that we will still be pen pals.

With lots of love,
Your friend,
Duaa

FREEDOMS

Duaa and Saumya were down to writing their final letters. They had walked a long, if fine line, from discussing hobbies to stone pelting and more. How liberating that a friendship of just over a month, now had the courage, trust and equanimity to consider the call for freedom: 'Azadi'. This Urdu word, that is simple to pronounce, with no complex sounds, but has many compounded meanings.

They had both heard it, on the streets of Srinagar and Delhi. At various protest marches in recent years, young men and women had made it their own. It was written on posters, sung in songs, cried out loud in passionate slogans.

But it always harked back to the Valley, its pulsating echo there forever causing anxiety. An echo that would literally find its way to university campuses in the country's capital Delhi.

In the winter of 2016, it reverberated in a protest for Kashmir in Delhi's Jawaharlal Nehru University (JNU), a space strongly influenced by Left politics and a vibrant centre for debates on myriad issues ranging from class, caste, gender to communalism, nationalism and patriotism. At this protest, some of the posters said, 'Against the judicial killing of Afzal Guru and Maqbool Bhat! In solidarity with the struggle of Kashmiri people for their democratic right to self-determination' and 'Cowardly acts like the judicial murder of Afzal Guru can never suppress the flames of Azadi in Kashmir!'

Mohammed Afzal Guru, a Kashmiri separatist convicted for masterminding an attack on India's Parliament in 2001, was hanged in Delhi's Tihar Jail on 9 February 2013.[86] Maqbool Bhat, widely believed to be the leader of the first generation of Kashmiri separatists, was also hanged in Tihar Jail on 11 February 1984.[87]

Both hangings were executed suddenly and families claimed they were not notified, denying them the chance of a last meeting.[88] This was criticized by some activists opposed to the death penalty, like Gautam Navlakha and writers like Arundhati Roy who felt Guru had not been given a fair trial.[89] In 2014, the Supreme Court clarified in another case that family members of a convict need to be informed after their judicial remedies have been exhausted and the scheduled date of execution declared.[90] After the hanging of Bhat and Guru, they were buried in Tihar Jail and their mortal remains not handed to their families. The two execution dates have since been observed as Martyrdom Days in the Valley where two empty graves are kept marked for them.[91]

It was on 9 February 2016 that posters with 'judicial murder' splayed on them were raised at the JNU protest.[92]

But if political statements and Twitter trends like #CleanUpJNU that followed later were any marker, that was not the popular view. It became a fight between the left- and right-leaning students' groups. The BJP's student wing Akhil Bharatiya Vidyarthi Parishad (ABVP) leaders spoke up against the protest. After their complaint, a university panel carried out an inquiry into the incident and found that objectionable slogans, many of which spoke of 'Azadi', were raised during the rally, though it could not attribute the sloganeering to specific individuals noting that 'masked outsiders were allowed to take over the event'.[93] Three student organizers of the rally, all from left-wing students' groups, had already been arrested by Delhi Police on charges of sedition. Kanhaiya Kumar, Umar Khalid and Anirban Bhattacharya were accused of inciting people to oppose the Indian government.

And some people were indeed angry. But not against the government, against the students. One of the three students, the JNU students' union president, Kanhaiya Kumar, was attacked by a group of lawyers waving Indian flags, chanting *'Vande Mataram'* (salutations to mother, where mother refers to Mother India), when he was being taken to court. Some journalists were also injured. The Supreme Court had to lay down guidelines for the bail hearing, asking the police to ensure such lawlessness does not happen again.[94] Kashmir observed a one-day shutdown in support of the arrested JNU students, a gesture of solidarity that went largely unreported in the press.[95] The students were eventually released on bail, but faced penalties like temporary expulsion from the university and fines.

It would only be four years later, a few months before the 2019 parliamentary elections, that the Delhi government would give a green signal to the police to file a chargesheet in their case, paving the way for a trial. Apart from the three

JNU student leaders, this chargesheet would specifically name seven other students, all reportedly residents of Kashmir studying in different universities outside the State.[96]

Chanting 'Azadi' was serious business. After his release, in March 2016, Kanhaiya Kumar gave a speech among his supporters in JNU clarifying his meaning of 'Azadi' and disassociating himself from any 'anti-national' slogans that were alleged to have been raised in the Kashmir protest. 'We are not seeking freedom from India, but in India from those plundering it,' he said to resounding applause. As TV channels beamed his speech live across the country, he followed it up with more slogans.[97] 'From hunger. From corruption. From brahminism. From patriarchy. From casteism . . .' And the hundreds of students listening raptly to him for almost an hour replied with gusto, in unison, 'Azadi.'

That speech inspired more than just the students listening and the TV audiences watching that night. Once shared online on social media platforms, it got millions of views.[98] And it inspired many songs. Popular dubstep artist Dub Sharma remixed the speech with a Punjabi folk tune. It was uploaded on YouTube, where he called it 'a tribute to the ongoing student movement in India. Only meant for educational purpose.'[99] He told the BBC, for him, 'Azadi' was about freedom of expression. His song would later inspire a Bollywood version in the film *Gully Boy*. Then there was a rendition by Kerala singer, Pushpavathy Poypadathu. She said that the chants reminded her of the caste discrimination she faced.[100] 'Azadi' had struck a chord.

What did the chant mean for the students in JNU? Why did they join in that chorus listening to the speech Kanhaiya made after his release from jail? Probably, it meant many things for many people. Some students held posters that said 'Justice for Rohith Vemula.' Rohith was a Dalit student who had taken his own life in January 2016 at Hyderabad University. Along with four other students, he had been suspended on a complaint by ABVP students. Eventually removed from their hostel rooms and Rohith's fellowship suspended, they were on a relay hunger strike.

Rohith used the Ambedkar Students Association flag to hang himself and left a note that said, 'My birth is my fatal accident' and that 'the value of a man was reduced to his immediate identity and nearest possibility. To a vote.'[101] His death sparked protests around campuses across the country and revitalized debates around caste discrimination.[102]

The deeply felt cry for 'Azadi' had always been seized by minorities of different hues, at different times—Dalit, Kashmiri, Adivasi, the poor, the working class, the peasants, the intelligentsia, the LGBT community and women. In December 2012, a year etched in our collective conscience, for the inhumane sexual violence inflicted on a young woman on a moving bus in Delhi, it made its way to the capital's streets. Young women and men were drawn out of their homes—in anger, disgust and hope. They marched to the capital's heart, India Gate, and asked for 'Azadi'. Tired of being blamed for the violence meted to them, women asked for the responsibility to be shifted to the aggressors, and for themselves, they wanted the freedom to be. To dream their dreams, to wear what they want, to travel where they wished at a time of their choosing with friends of their choice.

Jyoti Singh didn't survive the attack, and the protests continued into the cold January days of 2013, forcing amendments to broaden the definition, increase penalties and fix accountability of police and law-enforcing agencies in the existing laws dealing with sexual violence.[103] Some new slogans were born: *'Bekhauf Azadi'* (freedom without fear),[104] *'Baap se Azadi'* (freedom from patriarchy), *'Khap se*

Azadi' (freedom from feudal panchayat's diktats), and '*Shaadi karne ki Azadi, na karne ki Azadi*' (freedom to decide who to marry or stay unmarried). Women did not want security by compromising on their freedoms. They demanded both and more. From equal rights to freedom from fear.[105]

Feminists had always wanted freedom. The vocabulary of their songs and slogans had started using the term 'Azadi' a few decades earlier. Journalist Nirupama Dutt has written about dancing and chanting to 'the catchy beat of the Azadi number' at the Women's Studies Conference in West Bengal's Jadavpur University in 1991.[106] Women activists recount the range of issues the slogan covered at the time. So many battles and so many elusive freedoms. From patriarchy, violence and silence. Many to be fought with one's own mind and socially taught norms and responsibilities.

Feminist Kamla Bhasin said there was no copyright to the rhythmic chant of 'Azadi', but that everyone had the right to copy it.[107] She pointed to her sisters across the border, in Pakistan, for inspiring her from their use of the slogan in the 1980s where it was chanted in the hidden corners of bazaars and melas for fear of reprisals.

Pakistan was under a dictatorship then. General Zia-ul-Haq had taken over power in a military coup in 1979 and imposed martial law. One of the measures in his efforts to Islamize the judicial system were the Hudood Ordinances that remained in force long after his decade-long rule.[108] They dealt with many crimes including those against women, like rape and adultery. But any prosecution needed the presence of male witnesses to the crime, leaving women extremely vulnerable and helpless. As a result, thousands of women were jailed for committing 'honour' crimes instead of being able to access justice for being victims of sexual violence. Protests against the ordinance invited beatings by police and jail.

foreign investors found the region to be profitable enough to risk investment.[114]

All of this has exacerbated the already high unemployment challenge there. Especially among educated youth. The experience has been the same even in high potential areas like sports goods manufacturing. India's favourite sport, cricket had always benefited from the Kashmir willow, the tree that provides fine wood for making bats. Once sought after around the world for its high quality, it hasn't been able to retain its popularity and quality. Export revenues have gone down with lack of technology upgradation and skill development of growers and manufacturers in the state.[115]

One of the biggest economic tragedies is tourism. The region has an abundance of tourist destinations. The pilgrimage to the Amarnath caves (one of the four holiest shrines for Hindus) in Kashmir and Vaishno Devi shrine in Jammu. The desert-like mountainous landscape, serene lakes and Buddhist monasteries in Leh-Ladakh. And the romantic idea that the Valley with its breathtaking snow-clad peaks and lush green fields is like 'paradise on Earth', may have inspired many Bollywood films, calendars and coffee-table books, but has not been able to get Kashmir into the country's top ten domestic tourism destinations.

However, the region does not have stark deprivation. It does not report agrarian distress leading to farmer suicides and hunger deaths nor is it dotted with widespread urban slums.[116] Its expenditure on the health sector has seen year by year increase, infant mortality rate has had a declining trend and life expectancy rates have increased.

While the education sector has also seen increased investment by successive governments, the outcomes haven't always been as desired. For example, the then state government of Jammu and Kashmir attributed falling enrolment and rising dropout rates at upper-primary level from 2015–16 to 2016–17 to the youth-led unrest in that period.[117]

It has been more than a century since that hydropower plant that Duaa highlighted in her letter, to underscore her state's level of development before independence. The 9MW Mohra Hydro-electric Plant, developed as early as 1905, was among the first of its kind in the subcontinent.

The era Duaa is growing up in is different. Where the youth's demand for freedom is as vocal, if not more, than the right to development, education and jobs. In the past decade, she has seen that desire slowly burn, like charcoal in the warm earthen pot of kangris through the quiet spells of chil-e-kalan, only to become loud and deafening every other summer. A cycle of fire and ice. Repetitive because it persists. Because the more things change, the more they remain the same. Still, she is not tired. To Saumya's persistent question, she replies,

As I mentioned in my previous letter that we've become habitual of the situation here and if a person is habitual to a situation he does not feel tired.

Or maybe, if a person is able to rekindle hope, they continue to dream on, march on.

Delhi
8 June 2017

Dear Duaa,

I got your letter and I was elated when you invited me to Kashmir. But I won't be able to travel for the next two years as these years are very crucial for my career.

My family and acquaintances congratulated me after our letters were published as well. I am very excited to tell you that our letters on the website of BBC Hindi have been read by about 96,000 people. My friends also read the letters and they appreciated them too.

I was a little hesitant to ask you about the freedom of Kashmir, but I couldn't hide my curiosity and I really liked your reply. The kind of freedom that the Kashmiris want is something that the whole of humanity seeks. The newspapers are coloured with examples of cruelty and disgust—some days a drunken father beats up his son, other days the son beats up his aged father. A one-sided love leads to an acid attack or a lover brutally guns down his girlfriend.

I want to know more about the demand for freedom of Kashmir and that's why I want us to keep writing to each other. That will be great!

I believe that everybody has something special about them and that everyone has a talent to do something or the other, that's why everyone should have an equal chance to develop.

I was delighted to know that hospitals, schools and colleges were already there in the twentieth century in Kashmir.

I realized through our correspondence that young girls like us have very similar likes and dislikes. This project helped me to understand Kashmir in a new light and that Kashmir has developed in the way that I had expected it to. However, tourism gets affected from time to time due to the violence and it affects the everyday life of citizens too. I would like us to talk more about this.

The condition of the other states in India is as good as Kashmir when it comes to corruption and this definitely slows down development.

In the end, I would like to thank BBC for giving us a chance to meet this way and understand each other's perspectives.

I hope we keep writing to each other.

Lots of love,
Your friend,
Saumya

2019

PAST, PRESENT, FUTURE

Two years on, a lot had happened. In the summer of 2019, history was being written.

Narendra Damodardas Modi was sworn in as the prime minister of India for the second time in a row, the only non-Congress prime minister to retain power for a second term with full majority. This feat had earlier been accomplished only by Jawaharlal Nehru and his daughter Indira Gandhi. Modi's party, the BJP had swept the country in a resounding victory, winning 303 of the country's 542[118] constituencies.[119] This was an improvement in both number of seats won and vote share for the party from its first electoral victory in the Lok Sabha elections of 2014.[120] Ensuring that the BJP-led National Democratic Alliance, became the only non-Congress government to return to power after a full term in the Parliament, a second and even firmer stamp on the

Hindu nationalist party's ideas and vision. Tellingly, in his victory speech, Modi said, 'The political pundits of India have to leave behind their ideas of the past.' The present beckoned a new future. The country and its people seemed to have turned a corner.

Narendra Modi's personality towered over all else, even his party. According to a pre-poll survey, a third of the people who voted for BJP, did so looking at him and not the local candidate or party.[121] Not surprising, considering a fair bit of the party's campaign asked for votes in his name only. This, despite the fact that the impact of the economy's poor health was being acutely felt by the people. Unemployment was at its highest in almost half a century, as revealed by a government survey.[122] The invisible agrarian crisis that only gets noticed when farmers die was suddenly staring at us. Faced with drought and debt, many farmers had trekked to the country's capital in the run-up to the elections to make their voice heard, enabling their presence felt via news channels. And the controversial decision of demonetization in 2016 had broken the back of the vast unorganized sector, many still reeling under its after-effects. Yet, the leader and his party that had overseen the country on this path, was trusted to lead the country for the next five years. As he had, in the bloody winter just before the election.

It was the day the world, its markets and consumers have learnt to celebrate with love every year: 14 February, Valentine's Day. In 2019, as usual, news channels had a fair share of special coverage that ranged from love across caste and class boundaries, same-sex love, online-dating apps et al. Late in the afternoon, the first breaking news flashed. There had been an attack on the Srinagar–Jammu national highway in Pulwama district. At least twelve personnel of the CRPF were reported to be killed and many injured. Correspondents on the ground cautioned that these numbers could rise. Slowly, images and information trickled in. It emerged that this was a suicide attack. A car laden with explosives had been rammed by its driver into a bus in the CRPF convoy. The impact was so massive that not much remained of the vehicle.

By the time night fell, the death toll had risen to forty, making this one of the deadliest attacks on security forces in Kashmir in recent decades. There was an outpouring of grief from people across the country and a political outcry for revenge. In his first public comments, the prime minister made his intent clear, 'I understand that the blood of our people is boiling, there is an expectation to do something. The armed forces have been given full freedom.'[123]

By the following day, Pakistan-based militant group Jaish-e-Mohammed (JeM) had said it had carried out the attack and released a video of the suicide bomber, Adil Ahmed Dar. A high school dropout from Kashmir, he was twenty-two years old. His story was disturbing, for being so familiar. His family attributed his anger towards the Indian state to his getting badly injured in the protests that erupted after the killing of Burhan Wani in the summer of 2016. Adil's father said, 'That day changed him forever.' Shot in his leg, he was confined to bed for eleven months. Once he recovered, in early 2017, he left home never to return.[124] After the Pulwama attack, in his village in Kashmir, he was treated as a martyr. His funeral was attended by hundreds.

Home-grown militancy is different from cross-border terrorism. According to the home ministry, the number of young men joining militancy from within Kashmir has constantly been on the rise for a few years.[125] The militancy of the 1990s, which was encouraged from across the border, especially through training of young men and provision of arms, has been suppressed, but the scars remain on a younger generation that grew up witnessing the security forces' crackdown.[126] That continuing internal unrest provokes the youth that has found a community and platform on social media. Indoctrination is not happening across the border, but here at home. And cross-border aid has not disappeared—it has just found newer routes.

The government and the security forces have made efforts towards assimilation over the last two decades. To integrate Kashmiri youth with the rest of the country and instil trust and confidence—ranging from sports tournaments, cultural events to creating job opportunities and visits to meet the central political leadership. Kashmiri people themselves have also tried to build bridges. Some out of choice, and others for lack of opportunities in their region. By moving to different parts of the country for education and employment.

But it doesn't help the situation, when anger against militancy in the Valley is expressed against these Kashmiris in the rest of India. As it happened after the Pulwama attack.[127] In some incidents that got reported in the media, students were asked to leave their hostels, traders attacked while travelling on trains, tenants asked to vacate their rented accommodation.

This is a paradox of sorts. Because these Kashmiris—students, traders, even soldiers—are the ones who believed in assimilation with India. This is the reason they stepped out from the Valley, leaving distrust, anger and hopelessness behind. Being seen as a face of the militant in the Valley, and branded as traitor, anti-national or Pakistani, would shake that carefully built confidence. Instilling fear, taking them back home. Perpetuating the very cycle, they had set out to break. Two years before the Pulwama attack, when Saumya had asked Duaa about studying in any part of India outside

Kashmir, she had replied with these very apprehensions. She felt safer studying in another country, she wrote. Confident of being accepted among foreigners, as opposed to being attacked by some of her fellow citizens.

The Indian government was clear that Pakistan was behind the Pulwama attack as it harboured JeM. The group has been declared a terrorist organization not just by India but also by the UN, the US and the UK.[128] Pakistan denied these allegations. However, JeM continues to operate from its soil. It was founded by the Muslim cleric Masood Azhar after he was released in exchange for the passengers and crew of an Indian airliner hijacked in 1999. JeM is also alleged to have organized the attack on the Indian Parliament in December 2001 and on India's airbase in Pathankot in January 2016 that killed three security personnel.

That is not the only group Pakistan is accused by India of sheltering for fomenting unrest in Kashmir. In the months after Burhan Wani's encounter in the summer of 2016, militants executed an attack at the Indian army's brigade headquarters near Uri in September, killing nineteen soldiers. Most of the soldiers died in their sleep in this early morning attack allegedly carried out by Lashkar-e-Taiba (LeT).[129] An Islamist militant group, LeT was formed in the early 1990s and continues to operate from Pakistan.[130] It has been proscribed as a terrorist organization by the UN, the US, the UK and India. LeT was charged with organizing the 2008 Mumbai attacks that killed more than 160 people and the 2006 Mumbai train attacks[131] that killed about 190 people. It did not take responsibility for the Uri attack though, and JeM's name also came up at one point.[132] Pakistan again denied any involvement, pointing fingers instead at India for suppressing Kashmiri voices of dissent.

Public opinion in India was not amenable to these assertions. Prime-time television shows carried high-pitched debates about India's retribution after the Uri attack. Social media was abuzz with anti-Pakistan memes. Previously, India had never used military force in response to an attack by alleged Pakistan-sponsored militants. Instead, less confrontational channels—downgrading diplomatic ties, stopping trade, isolating Pakistan internationally—were adopted. Deterrence was the policy towards the nuclear power-enabled neighbour.

But not anymore. On the night of 28 September 2016, the Indian army crossed the LoC and launched what it termed a 'surgical strike' in Pakistan-administered Kashmir. India justified the strikes as a pre-emptive measure based on intelligence that Pakistan was planning an attack on its soil.[133] The number of fatalities was never put forth by India, but the director general of military operations, Lieutenant General Ranbir Singh said, 'terror launch pads' were hit in the strikes that caused 'significant casualties' to 'terrorists and those providing support to them'. No further details were made public. Pakistan denied this and dismissed the strikes as cross-border shelling. Claims and counterclaims on the extent of damage and fatalities were made by both countries. Some media reports suggested that 'the truth probably lies somewhere in the middle'.[134]

It seemed to suffice that some damage was done, a retaliation executed. Popular writer Chetan Bhagat tweeted, 'Looks like someone justified his chest size today. This is India. You don't mess with us. Ever. #surgicalstrike'.[135] He was not alone in expressing pride in India's leadership. [136] Many hailed the prime minister as a bold, decisive, daring leader. #ModiPunishesPak trended alongside #IndianArmy.[137]

Even the main opposition Congress party rallied behind the government's decision to strike back.[138]

The 2016 surgical strike inspired a Bollywood film. *Uri: The Surgical Strike* released in January 2019, three months before the parliamentary election. The film was a blockbuster success with earnings topping Rs 200 crore in India alone. Apart from a cinematic reference to how the surgical strikes may have been executed and the damage they might have caused, it also gave cine-goers a dialogue exchange between the hero, an army officer and his battalion. At key points in the attack and its preparation, he asks them, 'How's the *josh* (spirit or enthusiasm)?', to which they reply, 'High, sir.' Its popularity spread like wildfire, even the prime minister asked the question to an audience comprising the film fraternity, to get the same reply.[139]

Just over a month later, the dialogue would be used in a play of words with 'Jaish' replacing 'josh'. When JeM would take responsibility for the Pulwama suicide attack that killed forty Indian soldiers. Within a fortnight, on 26 February 2019 after India retaliated, just as it had after the Uri attack, launching a second 'surgical strike', the next day's newspapers would be splayed with headlines like, 'How's the Jaish? Destroyed, sir.'[140]

This second strike in 2019 was significantly different from the one in 2016. It was not a ground operation, instead executed by the Indian Air Force, the first aerial strikes since the 1971 war between India and Pakistan. They had a specific target: the biggest training camps of JeM. And the target was not just across LoC but inside Pakistan's territory.

India again stated self-defence as a justification. The foreign secretary Vijay Gokhale stated, 'Credible intelligence was received that JeM was attempting another suicide terror attack in various parts of the country, and the fidayeen jihadis were being trained for this purpose. In the face of imminent danger, a pre-emptive strike became absolutely necessary.'[141] The government claimed, 'In this operation, a very large number of JeM terrorists, trainers, senior commanders and groups of jihadis who were being trained for fidayeen action were eliminated.'[142]

Pakistan was prompt in sharing its own version of events. The military media wing of Pakistan armed forces tweeted that no infrastructure got hit, nor were there any casualties because of the Indian aircraft's 'intrusion'.[143] Pakistan's Prime Minister Imran Khan convened a meeting, after which a statement was released to suggest that the strike was done by the Modi government with an eye on the upcoming parliamentary elections in India. It said, 'Once again [the] Indian government has resorted to a self-serving, reckless and fictitious claim. This action has been done for domestic consumption, being in an elections environment, putting regional peace and stability at grave risk.'[144]

That might have been more of a warning than a defence. For all its allegations of an elections environment dictating India's actions, Pakistan had its own domestic constituents to consider. Two 'surgical strikes' by India, including the latest one inside its territory, did not exactly make the Pakistan government shine in the eyes of its own voters. The very next morning, after India's strike, Pakistan declared it had also carried out strikes across the LoC but from its own airspace, in response to which Indian aircrafts entered Pakistani airspace. Pakistan claimed two aircrafts were shot down and a pilot captured.[145] However evidence of only one Indian fighter jet being downed and its pilot missing, were eventually confirmed.[146] Pakistan released videos and images of Indian Wing Commander Abhinandan Varthaman in captivity.

After hours of hectic negotiations with India, Pakistan agreed to hand Wing Commander Varthaman back. Prime minister Imran Khan told his members of Parliament that the release was being done as a 'peace gesture'.[147] Indian news channels ran coverage of the expected release, as celebrations broke out across the country. Crowds gathered at the border in Wagah to witness what was being touted as a historic moment: when the pilot's return would mark the end of this escalation of hostilities between the two neighbours.

What continued as a subject of political analysis and debate was the claim that this escalation was just theatrics executed with an eye on gaining traction for the upcoming Indian elections, especially as ministers within the government kept giving high figures of casualties inflicted by Indian Air Force in the 'surgical strike'. The claim was questioned in many media reports. Some filed after visiting the location of the Indian strike, Balakot in Pakistan, and by comparing satellite images before and after the attack.[148]

Allegations about political motives were levelled by many Opposition leaders too, from the chief minister of Delhi to the main opposition Congress party. In a last-ditch effort as late as May, more than halfway into the seven-phase voting in the General Election, Congress even alleged that at least six surgical strikes had been carried out under the United Progressive Alliance (UPA) regime that they headed. The BJP disagreed, calling it a lie.

In the end, it did not matter. The year 2019 proved that 2014 was not an aberration. The majority in the country was willing to give their mandate to a government that was trying a different path. And as would quickly become clear in the next few months, one that would take everyone, whether they voted for it or not, into a very different direction.

It was difficult to say if the surgical strikes had had their intended impact. If the motive was revenge, then people's renewed confidence in the country's government suggested they were satisfied. But if the aim was to demonstrate the country's military capabilities to ensure deterrence from across the border on intrusions into Kashmir, then that did not seem to have hit the target. According to the home ministry's annual report, successful infiltration attempts had been increasing from 2016 (119), the year when Burhan Wani was killed and India launched its first 'surgical strike' in response to the Uri attack, in 2017 (136) and 2018 (143).[149] The figure in 2018 was the highest in the previous five years. Despite the fact that the number of terrorists killed in the years from 2014 to 2018, had also increased, 2019—the year which began with the second 'surgical strike' and in which history had been written in the summer—was only halfway through.

PART II

DIVIDED WE FALL

Almost two years after making first contact with Duaa, I finally went to Jammu and Kashmir in 2019. When I was in her state, I often thought of Duaa, and of her observing the various characters playing their parts in the play being enacted on the stage of Kashmir. Soon after the letter exchange got over in the summer of 2017, we had organized a live interaction between her and Saumya via Skype, which was broadcast over BBC Hindi's Facebook page. It was their first meeting, albeit virtual. Duaa had visited Delhi with her parents in 2018, and finally met Saumya and me in person. But after that, we had fallen out of touch. A message or an odd call aside, I hadn't properly spoken with her.

On 28 February 2019, I flew to Jammu when the country felt at the brink of war. News channels had been saying so since the Pulwama attack by JeM. India had done a surgical

There was also fatigue at every conversation centring around Hindu-Muslim or India-Pakistan. A Hindu woman shared some of the status updates that littered her social media feed: '*Aar paar ki ladai ka waqt aa gaya hai* (It is time to fight, to win or die) and '*Pakistan ko munh tod jawab dena chahiye*' (We should give a befitting reply to Pakistan). 'They are watching all this warmongering on TV, but do they realize what a war will mean for them, for us?' she asked.

But it was the observation of a Hindu man in that group that left me most disturbed. Of the mainstreaming of aggression that had happened over the past few years. He explained that Hindus in Jammu always pointed to Muslims in the Valley as troublemakers, supporting militancy, stone pelting, taking the law in their hands. But these very people, he pointed, had now allowed their children to be communalized and resort to violence. 'I think this was always inside them and has come out in the open now, because everyone is saying such things, even the prime minister and his ministers, so they know no action will be taken, they can get away with it,' he said.

The 1990s, when there was a rise in militancy in the Valley, was also the time when the rest of the country was witnessing the rise of the Hindu right. A pivotal moment was the demand for the construction of a temple at the small town of Ayodhya in Uttar Pradesh, believed to be the birthplace of Lord Rama, where a mosque, the Babri Masjid stood. The BJP joined the movement in 1989, started originally by the Vishva Hindu Parishad (VHP)[152]. In a concerted campaign, bricks marked with the name of Lord Rama were collected from around the country. This consolidation of the Hindu sentiment resulted in the BJP's first big electoral showing. From winning two seats in 1984, its first parliamentary elections after being formed in 1980, the party won 85 in the 1989 elections and became part of a coalition government at the centre.[153] Then BJP president L.K. Advani organized a 10,000 km Rath Yatra (Chariot Parade) in 1990 to further mobilize support. The yatra and the final act of a Hindu mob breaking the Babri Masjid in 1992, triggered communal riots. Retaliation and attacks across the country killed hundreds.[154] BJP's electoral gains continued, helping it stake its first claim at forming the government in 1996 (which lasted for only thirteen days), then in 1998 (thirteen months) and finally in 1999 when it lasted a full term.

These developments found an echo in Jammu and Kashmir too. After the Rath Yatra, the new BJP president Murali Manohar Joshi decided to embark on a Ekta Yatra (Unity Parade) to begin from Kanyakumari from the southern tip of India and culminate in Srinagar in the north, with Joshi hoisting the Indian flag at Lal Chowk on 26 January 1992. This was a formidable task, given the clout of militant outfits in the Valley at that time. The yatra was successful till Jammu where it had to be abandoned in the face of immense security threat. Murali Manohar Joshi, along with yatra convenor Narendra Modi, were airlifted to Srinagar, where at the heavily fortified Lal Chowk, guarded by the army, Joshi hoisted the flag with just about sixty supporters in tow and left in a matter of minutes.[155]

None of it was in vain. After the clampdown on militancy, when the erstwhile state of Jammu and Kashmir could participate in the Lok Sabha elections again in 1996, BJP registered its first win in the region with Udhampur. In the next elections in 1998, it won Jammu too. And in the 2014 elections, with a victory in Ladakh, BJP won three of the six parliamentary constituencies in the region. The other three (Baramulla, Srinagar, Anantnag) are in the Muslim-dominated Valley.[156]

I was in Jammu, headed to Hindu-majority villages near the LoC. Majid Jehangir was our guide and he ably led us to the villages at Zero Point in Naushehra sector of Rajouri district. Suddenly, our driver stopped the car and pointed me to the Indian army camp visible at a distance. I craned my neck out from the window, eventually gave up and stepped out of the car to get a view. Majid, at least one feet taller than me, stepped out too and asked me to tread carefully. He had spotted what I had missed. Straight ahead of me were some broken shells—small but still smouldering. It was the morning after an evening and night of shelling. All was quiet at the moment, but I felt a strange tension build up inside. We got inside the car and drove on to the next village.

Clad in flak jackets and helmets provided and mandated by the BBC for our personal protection, we must have looked nervous to the villagers who had witnessed shelling just the previous day, yet went about calmly in their regular clothes. But even if they felt it, they didn't make it evident. Instead, patiently showed us the damage to their house. Broken glass and cement were littered everywhere. They hadn't cleaned it up yet, waiting to show it to any local officials that may come by. A young girl peered at me from a hole in the wall, made by a bullet, but ran away as soon as she caught my eye. Her mother had been fatally hit by stray shells while filling water from a well a few years ago. A common occurrence here as people went about their lives, working in the fields or walking to school.

Young children played around us, collecting remnants of shells. A popular game, a girl told me; she hoped to win by collecting the most shells that day. I could see smoke coming out of the pieces she had gathered and asked her to throw them away and wash her hands with soap. But she just smiled and said, 'I am not scared, I will become a policewoman when I grow up. I don't feel fear.'

Police or armed forces are the most sought-after occupations in this mostly agrarian area with not many opportunities. Cross-border tensions, firing and curfews mean schools are often shut for long periods of time, making it difficult for children brought up on intermittent learning to compete with those in the cities in competitive exams and job interviews. One mother, whose son is in the army, said, 'This time it should be settled once and for all; it is time to fight, to win or die.'

But there was no war, no final settlement that would have decided Kashmir's fate once and for all. Pakistan agreed to return India's pilot Wing Commander Abhinandan Varthaman as a gesture of peace. India claimed it as their victory. Reports of cross-border shelling continued for a few more days even after I returned to Delhi. The pause button had been pressed. It would be status quo for the time.

Within a few months, I travelled to the region again. In June 2019, this time to the Kashmir Valley. But again, I wouldn't meet Duaa. I had gone to follow the case of an eight-year-old girl's brutal gang rape and murder which, after being politicized, had deepened existing religious fissures. It was a shocking crime against a child and an important story to tell, but it intrigued me also because the case lay bare the delicate relationship between two communities and the political context it had unravelled in.

The verdict was due in her case. Our difficult mission was to track her family that belonged to the Muslim nomadic tribe, Bakkarwals, as they trekked through the mountains in the restive Anantnag district. The Kathua rape and murder case, referred so after the place where the crime took place, had split the state on religious lines.[157] The girl had gone missing in Kathua in January 2018, when she had gone out to take horses for grazing. More than a week later, her battered body was discovered. Investigators arrested seven men accused of confining the child in a local temple for several days, sexually assaulting her and then bludgeoning her to death. The alleged crime was shocking, but soon acquired a communal colour. The arrests of Hindu men in the alleged rape and murder of a Muslim girl sparked protests in Jammu with two BJP lawmakers even attending a rally in support of the accused.

The BJP was part of the state government at that time, for the first time ever in Jammu and Kashmir. Their performance in the November–December 2014 assembly election, which saw the highest voter turnout in the state in twenty-five years, had been impressive.[158] But their wins, concentrated to the Jammu region, were not enough to form a government.[159] Eventually, they worked hard to be part of an unusual coalition, which took long months of negotiations to be finally strung together in March 2015. The BJP, a party that firmly believes in Kashmir being a part of India, was sharing power with the Peoples Democratic Party (PDP), a party formed by former Congress leader Mufti Mohammad Sayeed in 1999 with the promise of self-rule for the then state of Jammu and Kashmir.[160]

It was always going to be an unlikely partnership that had the potential to anger the traditional support base of both political parties. The coalition could not survive its full term. There was a rise in militancy in the Valley, the government heavily criticized for its handling of the civil unrest post

Burhan Wani's death in 2016 and the most immediate discord, over the extension of a ceasefire, or suspension of counter-insurgency operations, put in place during the month of Ramazan. In June 2018, BJP announced that it was pulling out of the coalition 'in the larger national interest of India's integrity and security' and 'the deteriorating security situation', and governor's rule was imposed.[161] But critics pointed out that this could be a politically motivated decision, taken with an eye on the 2019 parliamentary elections.[162] Other analysts suggested that the handling of the Kathua rape case by the coalition government was also a factor that made the BJP feel 'that Jammu was also slipping out of its hands'.[163]

The participation of BJP lawmakers in the rally supporting the accused in the Kathua case was widely criticized. It communalized the situation and divided people, damaging a carefully built balance between the Muslim nomadic tribe and the local Hindu residents. Once reported by media in the rest of the country, it prompted widespread protests demanding action against the ministers, leading to yet another political crisis in the state. With immense public pressure and some reportedly from the coalition partner PDP's leader, chief minister Mehbooba Mufti herself, the BJP ministers had to resign from their posts.[164]

The nomadic Bakkarwal tribe earn their living by selling livestock. In the summer months, they walk for days on end, hunting for pastures for fodder in the hilly areas of Kashmir. In the winter months, they move to the Hindu-dominated Jammu region. It was while they were here in January 2018 that the eight-year-old was assaulted in Kathua.

On the eve of the verdict in the case, almost a year and a half after the crime, the divisions felt fresh and raw—in fact, deeply entrenched, especially in the minds of young girls and women.

We trekked for a few hours on narrow roads, sand and gravel in bits and parts, and finally found them. It was a big group. When the Bakkarwals move, its mostly with the whole clan. The mother of the girl looked haggard and tired. Losing her daughter in that barbaric crime and then dealing with the communal fallout. She said she was always clear that she had to fight this. 'From the first day I knew, I would sell my animals if I needed to, use up all my savings, stay hungry, but get justice.'

On 10 June 2019, six of the accused were found guilty. Three were given life sentence, and three police officers were sentenced to prison for five years each. But for her other daughter and her cousins, this was not over. A religious divide had seeped in, one they never experienced before. They talked about a nagging fear of Hindu men that alienated them from long-standing friendships. One of them told me, 'I have so many Hindu girlfriends and I really miss them, but I don't go to their house anymore or talk to them; it is too painful.'

Saumya had messaged me just before I had travelled to the Valley for the Kathua verdict. She wanted to know where I had studied journalism! Eventually, though, she chose to do her bachelor's degree in English. Over the past two years, Saumya had stayed in contact. She didn't call, as she did not have her own phone but would message me sometimes on Facebook Messenger. Often, just to say hello and sometimes with something she wanted to share. Once, she messaged me an open letter she had written to a group of parents and teachers about exam pressure after a tuition mate died by suicide. It was a heartfelt, honest, polite but somewhat angry and frustrated letter. At other times, she would ask me about my work and remember the letter exchange fondly. I was curious if she and Duaa had kept in touch after that, and Saumya confirmed that they sometimes shared photos and wished each other on their important festivals. Like in June that year, she'd wished Duaa on Eid. Those were the last messages they exchanged in the summer of 2019. Before it all happened.

It started as a mix of rumours and official orders about Jammu and Kashmir being leaked on to social media in the last week of July 2019. Threats of an imminent terror attack started circulating as 10,000 paramilitary troops were flown in, in addition to the security forces already deployed in the Valley. People started stockpiling food and supplies in panic.[165] Slowly, an anticipation of a big announcement that could change the special status the state enjoyed, started building up. This was categorically denied on 30 July by governor Satya Pal Malik, who was in charge after the state assembly had been dissolved last year.[166] It had been a year since the BJP-PDP coalition broke up and some speculated that the troop movement might finally be in preparation for an election.

On 2 August, the state government issued an advisory for pilgrims on the Amarnath Yatra, to curtail their stay and leave the Valley immediately, 'keeping in view the latest intelligence inputs of terror threats'.[167] Special flights were arranged for their evacuation. On 3 August, countries around the world—including Australia, Germany and United Kingdom—issued an advisory against travelling to the state, again citing fear of violence and unrest.[168] On 4 August, Kashmir University postponed all exams scheduled from the following day with no fresh dates announced.

By then messages were circulating thick and fast via social media. It was hard to distinguish between fake news, speculation and facts. The whole political leadership, including former chief ministers Mehbooba Mufti (PDP)[169] and Omar

Some people in Delhi and the rest of India are talking about buying plots of land there and dreaming of marrying there despite the fact that they may not have enough to eat here or a place to live. People here are not understanding that now Kashmir will be left to industrialists and the damage that will cause will push the rest of the country towards natural calamities. What do you think about this? And how do Kashmiris view it?

Pardon me that I am asking you so many questions in my first letter itself. But these things have been bothering me a lot and probably no one could give me better insight than you.

Waiting for your next letter.

Your friend,
Saumya

Srinagar
30 December 2019

Dear Saumya,

A chilling salaam from Kashmir.

Chilling because it is really really, cold here these days. I am good and Alhamdulillah, everyone in my family is doing good. How are you and everyone in your family? We didn't continue on your promise of being 'pen pals' because of the fact that here, internet is down most of the time and staying in touch with anyone outside the Valley is a task in itself.

I was really happy to know that you've started college and your studies are going good. Mine, Aveen's or for that matter, studies of any student studying in Kashmir is suffering, really there is no other word for it. I just finished my Class XI board exams and now I am preparing for Class XII. I am the kind of student who believes in self-study and not the gag of coaching centres. People like me have suffered the most in the past few months, we used to study ourselves with some help from the magic of the internet. We used to consult the web whenever we had any doubts, but due to the unavailability of the internet, from the past few months our doubts remained doubts and only the Almighty knows how we've completed our syllabus in time to give our exams. I believe only Kashmiri students could face this scenario head-on and if students from the rest of Indian cities faced similar crisis, I am 100 per cent sure, they won't be able to bear it.

Shutting down of the internet and other telecommunications was all the result of scrapping of Article 370 of the Indian Constitution, J & K's special status. In a nutshell, I would like to tell you that people here are not happy with the removal of our special status. Personally, I feel depriving people to even talk to their near and dear ones is a violation of human rights. Machinery worth crores of rupees is on the verge of dysfunction in Kashmir's leading hospitals—most people here do not know what is going on in the world outside the Valley. All of this is due to unavailability of the internet. I feel it is a violation of human rights and right to information of people.

You talked about industrialization here, well most people do not know that many Indian industries like Union Carbide, Tata Steels, etc. had units in our industrial areas, but these units have been shut down long ago due to reasons more than one. Reasons mainly include geographical, topographical and varying political conditions here. So I feel industrialization on a large scale probably won't work here. You also said that people there are dreaming of marrying here. Well, dreaming about various things is human nature, but it is not necessary that all dreams come true.

Saumya, most people including myself do not understand as to what is going on in the rest of the country. News channels here do not give us enough information so as to understand what CAA and NRC really is. Can you brief me about it? All we get to hear is that there are protests going on in various cities of the country due to passing of this amendment act. Also, we get to hear slogans like, *'Chale the Kashmir ko Bharat banane, poore Bharat ko hi Kashmir bana diya'* (Out to make Kashmir a part of India, they have made India like Kashmir). Is the situation really that bad there? Hope you can answer these queries of mine. I really want to know.

Eagerly awaiting your reply.

Your friend,
Duaa

INDIA

In August 2019, when I tried to contact Duaa, it all came to a naught.

On paper, on 5 August 2019, Kashmir became a part of India the way it had never been earlier. There were no special protections or powers. But in practice, Kashmir felt farther than ever before.

The communication clampdown was so complete that one could not contact anyone there to find out what was happening. The internet was completely shut. Mobile phones were not working. Even landlines, in an unprecedented move, were dead. There seemed no way to get in touch with Duaa or anyone else in the region.

After hours of deafening silence, our reporter on the ground somehow found a functional landline in a dhaba near the airport, contacted us late in the evening and shared the mood among people there.[173] Of complete uncertainty, fear and an overwhelming feeling of loss. It was an unannounced curfew. People inside their homes. Security forces omnipresent outside.

The additional troop deployment to the region in the week prior to the government's announcement removing the region's special status, had been done with an eye to deal with any fallout. Protests by people, attacks by militants or unrest fomented from across the border. It was a momentous decision, planned carefully by the government, and stunned everyone else.

The special status had been painstakingly negotiated in the 1950s as the terms for the Muslim-dominated state to remain with secular India instead of Islamic Pakistan after the country's partition. In 1952, Sheikh Abdullah, then prime minister of the state, had multiple meetings with then prime minister of India, Jawaharlal Nehru and his ministers to negotiate the Delhi Agreement, which gave more autonomy to the state, including among other provisions, a separate state flag, in exchange for Kashmiris to become full citizens of India.[174] But this did not enjoy support throughout the state. Differences between the Valley and Jammu became stark. The Praja Parishad, which represented the Hindus of Jammu, led agitations opposing the special status. Party workers would often climb atop government buildings to remove the state flag hoisted there. They found support in Dr Syama Prasad Mukherjee, founder-president of Bharatiya Jan Sangh. He wrote to the Central government and organized protests in Delhi in support of the demands of Praja Parishad. In 1953, he decided to take his satyagraha to the state itself, but was arrested as soon as he crossed the border and taken to Srinagar. Within six weeks in prison, he passed away.

His death was marked by massive protests in Jammu and in Kolkata, his hometown.

In 1954, the Delhi Agreement was adopted as The Constitution (Application to Jammu and Kashmir) Order, 1954 that specified the terms under Article 370 and Article 35A.[175] Under these, the state had its own Constitution and it could bar any Indians born outside the state from buying property there. Certain subjects like foreign affairs, defence and communication remained with the centre, but the state had relatively more freedom than the country's other states in making its laws.

Sixty-five years later, on 5 August 2019, The Constitution (Application to Jammu and Kashmir) Order, 2019 superseded the 1954 order and stated that 'all the provisions of the Constitution' will now onwards apply to the state of Jammu and Kashmir.[176] The Parliament witnessed angry scenes as the home minister, Amit Shah moved the Presidential Order and the reorganization bill to be passed. Some members walked out, a few voted against, but finally with the support of certain regional parties, the government had the numbers it needed.[177]

The state, which was under governor's rule for more than a year, was immediately reorganized into two union territories. Kashmir, it was declared, had truly become part of India now.

On 6 August, a petition was filed in the Supreme Court challenging the Central government's decision removing special status, arguing that it was illegal as it was done without the consent of the Jammu and Kashmir state assembly.[178] Over the following days, several petitions would be filed on that question of constitutional validity and would be clubbed together to be heard by a five-judge bench of the Supreme Court. The beginning of a long judicial process of scrutiny.

In the public court of opinion, the Central government's decisions were widely welcomed in the country, and were not wholly unpopular in the state. In a televised address to the nation, Prime Minister Modi called it a new beginning and hailed it as a dream of the country's leaders including Sardar Patel, B.R. Ambedkar and Dr Syama Prasad Mukherjee.[179] He promised better employment opportunities, reduction in revenue deficit and more development. He also said that the union territory status would be temporary till the Central government was able to assure free and fair elections. There were murmurs of support, though later, in hushed voices, some did voice concerns about the ban on outsiders buying property being removed, fearing loss of land and jobs. But not at that time.[180]

Kashmiri Pandits, who were forced to flee the Valley in the 1990s fearing militant attacks, hailed the announcement. However, the Muslim-dominated Valley had an overriding different sentiment. Having been promised a plebiscite under the Constitution, this unilateral decision was called unjust by many. The first protests were reported from Srinagar, after prayers on 9 August, the first Friday following the announcement. Thousands marched, some waving Pakistan flags and calling for 'Azadi'. Security forces opened fire and used tear gas to disperse the crowd.[181] But this was only reported by a few international news outlets.[182][183] The government initially denied any protests took place, later admitting that 'miscreants mingled with people returning home after prayers at a local mosque' and asserting that 'law enforcement authorities showed restraint and tried to maintain law and order situation' while reiterating that no bullets were fired.[184] The Valley was almost an information black hole.

The communication clampdown meant news and evidence was very difficult to collect. On 10 August, the executive editor of *Kashmir Times*, Anuradha Bhasin, filed a petition in the Supreme Court demanding that restrictions on internet and communications be lifted and curbs on journalists' movement be relaxed.[185] She contended that the restriction on information sharing at a time when the region was going through tumultuous changes was fuelling panic and fear.

Journalists could not contact people via phone calls to set up meetings or check availability. Nor were updates and information available online in the absence of internet. For everything, they had to physically travel to different parts of the region to verify information and gather people's opinions. In the absence of any communication lines, it was difficult to gauge threats and plan travel accordingly. Then, it was even harder for them to send the material they were able to gather, to their head offices from where it could be broadcast to the rest of India. The lack of access to emails, social media, online services and phone connections made that simple task painfully tough.

I had started presenting BBC Hindi's Radio programme *Din Bhar*, specially extended by half an hour to enable wider coverage of the fallout of the Kashmir developments. Making the programme at our Delhi office now included the challenging task of coordinating with our reporters on the ground, waiting for them to find a functioning landline and call us, grabbing the only opportunity to record the reports they had gathered.

Eventually, the government set up a press centre in Srinagar, from where journalists could access the internet and send emails, but there were long queues and poor connectivity. Many media organizations started sending someone on a flight from Delhi only to pick up and physically bring back information and video files, to be edited and broadcast, which often delayed the circulation of the news.

Lack of transparent communication led to anxiety and fears. As all mainstream regional party leaders, including three former chief ministers, had been put under house arrest or detention, leaders from other political parties in Delhi demanded the Central government allow them to visit the Valley to take stock of the situation themselves.[186] A group of human rights activists independently travelled to the Valley and released their findings in a report called, 'Kashmir Caged'.[187] It documented accounts of young boys and men being picked up by security forces and kept in illegal detention. The activists also showed pictures of two pellet gun victims of the first Friday protest and complained of not being given access to others they suspected were admitted in a hospital. The report detailed widespread resentment and desire to protest, suppressed under fear. Finally, it highlighted the difficulties local journalists were facing in doing their jobs freely and fairly.

Some investigative news stories filed with great difficulty by international news outlets echoed the findings of the 'Kashmir Caged' report. A BBC report recorded testimonies from a mother about her son being picked up at gunpoint and from a wife about her husband being taken to a jail outside the Valley, in Uttar Pradesh's capital Lucknow.[188] A Reuters report detailed mass detentions after the announcement. Of the thousands, as per the report, the majority were 'stone pelters and miscreants'.[189] According to the government, the detentions were to prevent protests and clashes that could cause loss of limb and life. Another BBC report had testimonies from several villagers who said they were beaten with sticks and cables and given electric shocks by security forces.[190] They felt it was done to intimidate them so they did not dare to protest or resort to stone pelting. The Indian army called the accusations 'baseless and unsubstantiated'.

Meanwhile, the government was trying to restore confidence and bring some relaxations in the clampdown. In his Independence Day speech, Modi reiterated the justification for the government's decision—that separatism and militancy had been a hindrance in development and people had gone astray.[191] Underscoring the support to it, that both houses of Parliament had passed the Presidential Order revoking special status and the Jammu and Kashmir Reorganization Bill 2019 bifurcating the state into union territories with two-thirds majority. And repeating his own party's commitment, that this step was taken within seventy days of the National Democratic Alliance coming into power. He used the slogan, 'One nation, one Constitution', harking back to the protest of the 1950s when Praja Parishad had opposed the special status chanting, *'Ek desh main do vidhaan, do pradhan, do nishan— nahi chalenge, nahi chalenge'* (One country cannot have two Constitutions, two heads of state and two flags).

On 19 August, some teachers and principals opened schools, but very few students turned up. Parents said they were scared for their children's safety and complained of lack of public transport to safely get them to schools and back.[192] So schools stayed open and students stayed away. Colleges and universities remained shut. Weddings were postponed or cancelled; tourism and trade suffered. The administration announced that shops could be reopened, but many didn't.

Later, Duaa would call it a 'lockdown', a term that would become familiar in the context of the Covid pandemic of 2020. But for Duaa, it was her fourth one. The first was in 2008, when she was six years old, and then in 2010 and 2016. She was familiar with the loss of school time, friends and freedoms. 'I was like a little princess growing up,' she said. 'My parents or the rest of my family never used to discuss anything about the armed forces in my presence and also little kids are so involved in their own world, they hardly care about what is going on.' All she wanted to recount was an acute sense of being constrained. Duaa called herself lucky, that she was born after the worst decade had passed and grew up in the new millennium in a protected environment. But insisted that many other or older children have been suffering deep scars of the mental stress of living amidst curfews and constant conflict.

I called and messaged repeatedly all through August to check on Duaa's family and well-being. But all attempts were futile. Saumya struggled too. In the two years since the letter exchange in April–May 2017, Saumya and Duaa had not been in touch regularly. Apart from that one meeting when Duaa visited Delhi, life had taken over and their promise of continuing as pen pals had fallen through. Saumya told me they messaged each other sometimes, but only on Snapchat and Instagram, and mostly pictures. The last time they interacted was to wish each other on Eid in June.

I could not go to Kashmir at this time. After presenting BBC Hindi's radio programme for two weeks, I was due to present another radio programme, *OS* on the BBC World Service from September, from the BBC's main newsroom in London. And it was while I was working from London that the communication restrictions in the Valley started getting lifted slowly. First it was some landlines, then some post-paid mobile phones. But it was still very difficult to make contact, especially on an international phone call. Even to connect to our reporter in Srinagar, we had to attempt a conference call via our studios in Delhi. The internet was still blocked, so the option of using messaging apps like WhatsApp did not exist. But at least there was a possibility now. In November, my editor Rupa Jha called from Delhi and we decided to explore the possibility of reviving the letter exchange between

Duaa and Saumya. She cautioned me that the situation had become much worse since 2017 and we will have to be very careful, keeping the safety of the girls foremost in our minds.

Things were far from normal in Kashmir. In October, the Indian government published a full-page advertisement on the front page of the newspaper *Greater Kashmir*.[193] It read, 'CLOSED SHOPS, NO PUBLIC TRANSPORT? WHO BENEFITS? Are we going to succumb to militants? Think!!!' There was anxiety, but there was also anger and fear. The Valley still had a huge security presence, political leaders (except of the BJP) remained under house arrest,[194] and thousands of young men were detained. The internet and mobile phone networks were still not working, though there was a slow and limited restoring of telephone lines.

I first messaged Saumya on Facebook Messenger, the app we used to communicate. It was life as usual in Delhi. A few weeks since Diwali and winter was setting in. Saumya was in the first year of college. The mention of Duaa got her excited: 'I miss the letter days, we both remembered them often . . . Duaa used to say, if it had continued, you would have kept asking me more questions ☺.' Saumya was thrilled to do a second round of letters, and this time Kashmir-related developments were clearly on her radar. On hearing that phone lines were functional, Saumya called Duaa right away. Within minutes, she reported that Duaa was on board too.

But this was a chat I needed to have with Duaa's parents. Saumya had turned eighteen, but Duaa was still seventeen and her parents' consent to her participation had to be secured. From London, it took me a couple of days and at least a dozen attempts to be able to connect with Duaa's father. When I finally heard a ring at the end of the line, it felt nothing short of a victory. His cheerful voice greeted me from the other side. Duaa's father, pleasantly inquiring about me and my family's health, as always. As if nothing had changed and we had spoken just the previous day. I didn't ask much, though I had so many questions. They were living through difficult times and I knew phone conversations were still not considered safe. So, we stuck to discussing the letters project. They readily agreed and the phone was handed to Duaa. She sounded different, more assured, confident and direct: 'I would love to write letters again, I am grown up now and understand what is happening around me much more clearly.' In December 2019, Saumya finally reconnected with Duaa with a letter from Delhi to Srinagar.

Clearly, the letters would tell a different story this time around. The girls knew each other now and understood and engaged with their realities much more. They were hungry to know and eager to tell. Duaa was a window to Kashmir, from where information had only slowly started trickling now. And Saumya was the storyteller of the rest of India. Out of reach for the still disconnected Valley, impatient to find voices they could trust. The letters turned out to be longer and more passionate. These were young women. Their views more considered, their words sharper, forthright. No more observers, but active participants. Forming and firming their own world view.

It was also a much slower process. With no access to internet, Duaa's letters couldn't be simply emailed to me nor could I send her Saumya's letters directly. It became a circuitous chore, enabled only for the kind help extended by our reporter, Majid Jehangir in the Valley. Always forthcoming and gracious to my requests made across time zones and continents this time. I would email him Saumya's translated letter. Then call him to let him know I had done that. He would then go to the government set-up Media Centre, queue up, wait for his turn, access his email, print the letter out and deliver it to Duaa. The same drill repeated itself once Duaa had written her reply. He would pick up Duaa's letter, go to the Media Centre, queue up, wait for his turn, scan the letter and email it to me. For all the reading, interviewing and presenting I had done over the past four and a half months on the Kashmir clampdown, the letter exchange taught me a significant lesson. Of patience, slowing down and waiting.

Delhi
12 January 2020

Dear Duaa,

I am fine, and everyone at home is also good. It is quite cold in Delhi too, but the mood is really hot.

I don't know how much you know about CAA and NRC, so I'll explain these two things the way I understand them. So CAA says that refugees from Afghanistan, Bangladesh and Pakistan living in India will get citizenship if they are Hindu, Sikh, Buddhist or Jain. But not if they are Muslims and Christians.

Secondly, NRC means that just as it happened at the time of demonetization, the public would be made to stand in queues to prove they are citizens of this country and that their ancestors' names have appeared in voter lists. I think very few people will have documents to prove that and to get those proofs, they will have to get in long lines. Those who are unable to get the documents, their citizenship will be suspended and they won't be able to open bank accounts, get government subsidies, government jobs, and that I think is very wrong. That is why protests are happening here.

Has Kashmir seen some impact of this law as well?

A few days ago, I went to the protest at Delhi's Shaheen Bagh. If you don't know about this protest, let me tell you that women have been protesting against this act there for the past twenty-six days. These women are not university professors or activists, but homemakers, women who remain in purdah, but have stepped out on to the streets to protest now. The protest at Shaheen Bagh becomes even more beautiful when one spots five-year-old girls to eighty- or ninety-year-old women there. Have you heard of 'dabang dadiyan'?

These are ninety-year-old women who are at the forefront of these protestors. They are fighting this battle so their children are able to lead their lives in peace. After witnessing the enthusiasm among the people at Shaheen Bagh, I'll say that people are prepared to fight this battle. This fight that we are fighting for our rights. The whole dharna at Shaheen Bagh is led by women. Do such women-led protests happen in Kashmir too? Would the protest at Shaheen Bagh show the way for Kashmir's women too?

On 5 January, when I was returning from Shaheen Bagh, I read this news on the internet that some masked goons had entered JNU's campus and attacked students there. JNU (Jawaharlal Nehru University) is one of India's top universities. The fee is really low here, so students from villages can also access education. One month ago, the university increased the fee. And where students were giving Rs 20, now they have to give Rs 150. The students' union opposed this and is still protesting against it. On 5 January, when protests were happening there, some masked goons got inside and attacked students, including a life-threatening attack on Jawaharlal Nehru University Students' Union (JNUSU) president Aishe Ghosh, who was hit with an iron rod on her head. And later, an FIR was filed against her only because the university wants to end this protest movement. And even after a week since the violence in JNU, there is no trace of those masked goons. I believe that violence by anyone is wrong and we will not accept such violence.

In your last letter, you had written that you've heard slogans like *'Chale the Kashmir ko Bharat banane, poore Bharat ko Kashmir bana diya'* were being chanted in Delhi. You are 100 per cent right. Since this protest movement started, all of Delhi is feeling like Kashmir. Like internet/phone shutdowns, Section 144 being imposed, stone pelting and police lathicharge during protests. So I can say that today I quite well understand Kashmir and the situation people living there are facing.

At the end I'd just like to quote a shayar: *'Kiske roke ruka hai savera, raat bhar ka hai mehmaan andhera'* (Who has been able to stop the dawn, darkness is only an overnight guest), and in the midst of this darkness, the student- and young people-led movement is the sign of a new dawn.

Waiting for your next letter.

Your friend,
Saumya

Srinagar
23 January 2020

Dear Saumya,

I was really shocked when I heard the news of the attack on JNU students. To be honest, I am afraid to turn on the news these days because whatever is going on in the country is not just shocking but also heartbreaking. From what you said about CAA and NRC, I feel we are going back in time instead of moving forward. I still can't believe that even in the twenty-first century some people discriminate others on the basis of caste, religion and in some parts of the society even gender. These practices need to be eliminated from our society; only then will we be capable of calling ourselves 'modern' or even 'broad-minded'.

Protests against CAA and NRC, I feel are completely genuine and these protests are a proof that people still believe in taking a stand for each other and that humanity is still alive. Unlike the rest of the Indian cities, Kashmir has been really calm about this act. In our hearts we know that this act is wrong, but these days we Kashmiris couldn't care less about what is happening outside the Valley. So no protests here. Even if we want to raise our voices, we know that they will be curbed. Our voices, our rights have been neglected in the past and are being neglected right now.

A couple of days ago, a NITI Aayog member V.K. Saraswat defended the communication ban and he went as far as saying that Kashmiris do nothing but watch 'dirty films' online. He also said that shutting internet down didn't have any significant impact on the economy. Well, to us common people over Rs 18,000 crore is a very huge amount, but it seems that it is not a significant enough amount for the authorities. Even though, he apologized later, these remarks cannot be just thrown out of our minds. Do people there really think that way about us? Do Kashmiris have no right over communication services? No one is talking about the problems that we are facing right now due to the internet ban. Are we really invisible to the rest of the country?

You wanted to know about Kashmiri women. Well, Kashmiri women are a force to be reckoned with. If it wasn't for them and their courage back in the 1990s, today Kashmir would have been just another prison for us. Today, the only thing holding us down is our love for our families. Here, if we people speak out, our families are troubled, which is the reason why most of us do not speak out anymore. But it doesn't mean that we can't and it for sure doesn't mean that we won't if the need arises.

Saumya, now that it is nearly 26 January, I want to know does Delhi undergo that excess checking thing. I know that it is an important thing to do, but does this excess checking and all the precautions taken at this point of the year ever trouble the studies of young children? Have the coaching centres ever been forced to close down at least a week before Republic Day? Well, here in Kashmir it seems like it is the new 'trend' among the authorities because our tuition centres have been forced to shut down a week before the national holiday. Our studies have already suffered a lot from the past almost six months. Winter break is going on in our schools and due to the unavailability of the internet, most students have taken to coaching centres to compensate for the loss that they have faced. In such a situation every hour counts in terms of studies, and students can't really afford that many holidays. Today it is in the name of 26 January, tomorrow it will be 14 February (Pulwama attack anniversary). Do you think it is just to put education on hold for a national holiday?

Waiting for your reply.

Duaa

REBELLIONS

It was a reversal of roles: Duaa was asking the questions; Saumya was the purveyor of her city and her country's story. Their stories and their lives seemed to overlap in a strange way. For some time in December 2019 and January 2020, many parts of the country had phone services suspended, internet shut, curfew imposed. Protestors faced tear gas and batons; the streets filled with youth and passion.

But these protesters were not asking for freedom from India, they were asserting their right to belong to this nation, to be an Indian, a bona fide citizen, of India, a secular republic. Where religion did not determine nationality nor had ever been the basis for its denial.

The fear was that was going to change. That a new law and a government-mandated register could together be used to endanger the citizenship of Indian Muslims. The purpose of the National Register of Citizens (NRC) was to make a list of Indian citizens and identify illegal immigrants, while the Citizenship Amendment Act (CAA) made it possible for certain illegal immigrants to get Indian citizenship. Hindus, Sikhs, Parsis, Buddhists, Jains and Christians from Pakistan, Afghanistan and Bangladesh could get amnesty if they could prove that they were fleeing religious persecution as minorities in those countries.[195] Muslims were not included in this provision, leading to apprehensions that the Hindu nationalist government would use CAA-NRC to marginalize Muslims in India.

The government reasoned that the CAA was brought in to give asylum to religious minorities in the three neighbouring Islamic countries and that it would not impact Muslim citizens of India. But the stakes, a possible loss of citizenship, were very high. The NRC had only been implemented in the north-eastern state of Assam to check illegal immigration from neighbouring Bangladesh. It tried to identify those who were living in the state on or before 24 March 1971, i.e. before Bangladesh was created, to declare them legal citizens.[196] When the final list of citizens was published on 31 August 2019, almost two million names didn't make it, exposing those people to possible detention or deportation. In many instances, some members of a family matched the citizenship criterion while others were declared illegal.[197] In December, Home Minister Amit Shah announced in a state elections campaign rally that the NRC would be rolled out across the country before the 2024 parliamentary elections,[198] but left it ambiguous which documents would be needed to prove citizenship.

The Citizenship Amendment Bill was passed by both houses of Parliament on 10–11 December 2019. Protests started spreading through the country, with students at the forefront. But within days, these peaceful protests started turning into battles as the police tried to disperse them using tear gas, rubber bullets and batons. Videos of police excesses at campuses filmed by students, like the one where a group of young women physically shielded their friend as he was attacked by baton-wielding policemen[199], started circulating. First it was Jamia Millia Islamia[200] in Delhi, where police could be seen entering a library and clashing with students studying there, and then at the Aligarh Muslim University[201] in Aligarh. At least fifty students were injured and dozens detained. But the protests reconvened and found widespread support from students of other educational institutions, who were joined by civilians in large numbers. The prime minister tried to assuage concerns about the law being anti-Muslim: 'I want to unequivocally assure my fellow Indians that CAA does not affect any citizen of India of any religion. No Indian has anything to worry regarding this act.'[202]

Saumya was drawn in. She would later tell me that at that time she felt, 'if the youth didn't think of the nation and take responsibility, who would?' With like-minded students, she would sit at the *chai ki tapri* (tea stall) outside her college, and sing poems penned by revolutionary poets—of equality, opposing state repression and authoritarianism.

When the CAA-NRC protests started, she believed that students needed to show solidarity to the struggle. Some of her friends were part of left-wing student groups like All India Students Association (AISA) and Students' Federation of India (SFI). They would pool in money, ask teachers for donations and organize protests in the college and outside. The only girl in a group of boys, she became a familiar face at protests and known in her college as 'the girl who is always found with boys'. Saumya said it felt like being in the middle of something very important, like a revolution.

Thousands of miles away, in London, I woke up every day five and a half hours behind Delhi, and scoured my social media feeds for the latest. Informing myself of the arguments for and against the government policy as I got ready for our daily news programme, to explain what was happening in my country to the world. The last time I had witnessed young people lead such large-scale protests across the country was in December 2012. The gang rape of a college student on a moving bus in Delhi had galvanized men and women, uniting in protest, eventually building enough pressure on the government that led to the strengthening of laws on crimes against women.

This was different. Opinions were sharply divided. #IndiaSupportsCAANRC trended on Twitter almost as much as #IndiaAgainstCAANRC, as supporters and detractors of the law fought pitched battles from their positions. Inflexible, almost set in stone, informed by years of experience and belief. Even the prime minister's personal website asked people to support a hashtag in support of the government's law.[203]

If one looked outside one's own bubble, beat the algorithm and broke out of echo chambers, it was clear that popular opinion remained with the government and its leader. One survey claimed that the majority of respondents did not believe the law was discriminatory against Muslims and would only leave out illegal immigrants.[204] The fear of being overrun by 'outsiders' was greater than the commitment to upholding secular ideals. Despite the revolutionary songs being sung at protests, mesmerizing scenes of hundreds chanting the national anthem together[205] and public readings of the country's Constitution, harking to equality and amity, India remained divided.

A definite anxiety and fear was creeping up among Muslims.[206] Not just poor Muslims who feared they did not have enough documentation to prove their citizenship, but also more privileged ones. When I met Indian Muslim friends working in London as their families visited from India during the December holiday season, the conversation mostly centred on what was happening back home. Some even considered moving permanently to the UK or US for a safer future or sending their children abroad to study, while others made light of the uncertainty. I remember one friend's dark humour when discussing the fallout of not being able to prove one's citizenship. He said, 'Don't worry, even if we lose our home, there is one place reserved for us—the detention centres.'

The protests continued. There were reports of buses being torched, an attempt to set fire to a police station. But there were also candlelight processions, and peaceful reading of the Indian Constitution. Thousands were detained, including non-violent protestors such as historian Ramachandra Guha, among others.[207] Section 144, which prohibits the assembly of more than four persons at one place, was invoked in various cities, while mobile services and internet were shut. This prompted Duaa to make the comparison with Kashmir, where protests were often curbed by shutting down communication lines.

As the rebellious days stretched on, a series of news reports started trickling in from Uttar Pradesh. Of policemen firing at stone pelting protestors breaking CCTV cameras on shops in Muslim localities, even vandalizing homes, looting cash and jewellery. More than twenty people died in the state, reportedly with bullet injuries.[208] Police denied they fired first, saying they were faced with armed protestors and that they had to go inside houses to make arrests. The state government issued an order to recover the cost of damage to public property during protests from the protestors themselves.

Protestors were identified and photos of their faces plastered on a hoarding with the sign 'Wanted' next to them.[209]

In the midst of these heated confrontations, a small group of women had started making their presence felt in the bitterly cold wintry nights on the streets of Delhi. The protest site in Shaheen Bagh, in a predominantly Muslim locality, was populated by working women, housewives, young girls, small children and grandmothers. All of whom had stepped out, breaking the traditional notions that a Muslim woman's place is inside the house. And their motivation were other Muslim women.

They spoke of the police action in Jamia Millia Islamia University.[210] Of the 'fearless' women at the forefront of those clashes, whose experiences were documented by a fact-finding team in their report titled, 'Unafraid'.[211] And of the women students at Aligarh Muslim University who braved batons, tear gas and sat alone or in twos to continue protesting after a round of pushback. They spoke of their shock and horror at the police excesses at those campuses and of their duty to protest and defend the democratic rights of their children.

Slowly, the numbers at Shaheen Bagh grew. The women from the locality took turns. Christmas Eve turned into New Year's, but the protest site was always full of women 24/7. They were a powerful image—very different from the stereotypical burqa-clad Muslim women seen in mainstream news media. They spoke, they had opinions. And they asked simple straightforward questions of the state.

Shaheen Bagh was an awakening of sorts for Muslim women. The hitherto invisible was becoming the visible strength of the CAA-NRC protests. Like the stone pelting women in Kashmir, who stepped into a form of protest that had till then been owned by men.[212] Muslim women had earlier been seen as bystanders to the rebellion in the Valley, looking down to the streets from the windows of their houses. Or seen as victims of violence, or mourners of their men who had become victims of violence. Now, they were actors.

For Duaa, this new image could not take away from the role Kashmiri women had played in the space traditionally demarcated for them, inside their houses. When Saumya wrote to her about the women from Shaheen Bagh inspiring Kashmiri women, she replied:

> You wanted to know about Kashmiri women. Well, Kashmiri women are a force to be reckoned with. If it wasn't for them and their courage back in the 1990s, today Kashmir would have been just another prison for us.

I later asked her to elaborate what she meant. She told me that the prison she was referring to was the prison of the mind that was not educated. She called it *'jahalat ki qaid'*. For Duaa, the women of Kashmir were the 'unsung heroes' in the Valley's 'dark history of the 1990s'. When their menfolk 'disappeared', women braved fear and violence, and made sure their 'children got a good education, were well fed—and that is what brought development to the region'.

It was important to acknowledge women in those roles in Kashmir. Of mothers, sisters and daughters. Women were speaking then too. Without mincing words. Their truth to power. Like when they would glorify those killed by the Indian army, 'celebrate them as martyrs' by singing the traditional songs of celebration, *wanwun*.[213] Or when the women in the villages of Kunan and Poshpora spoke and made sure FIRs were registered for the rapes they alleged the Indian army had inflicted on them. Or when women demanded information from authorities and led the fight to find the men of their families who had 'disappeared'. Like Parveena Ahangar did when her son 'disappeared' in 1990.

The United Nations defines 'enforced disappearance' as an 'abduction or detention of a person against their will by a government or by organized groups or private individuals at the behest of the government, followed by a refusal to disclose their whereabouts, which places the person outside the protection of law.'[214] With the help of legal professionals and activists, Parveena Ahangar, whose son 'disappeared' in 1990, founded the Association of Parents of Disappeared Persons (APDP) in 1994.[215] On the tenth of each month, families of the 'disappeared' hold a public protest in Srinagar, organized by APDP, to demand information about them. That is more than 300 months of protesting. Many of the women who gather, call themselves 'half-widows half-wives', believing that their husbands are alive but not knowing anything for certain.

According to APDP, more than 8000 people have 'disappeared' in Kashmir since the 1990s. The National Human Rights Commission issued notices to the state government and the central home and defence ministries at different points of time, seeking information.[216] In a written reply to the state assembly in 2017, the state government, under Mehbooba Mufti stated, '4088 missing people (of J & K) and terrorists are still in Pakistan and PoK,'[217] implying that all the disappeared persons had crossed the border and taken up arms during the 1990s. The APDP strongly refutes this and has documented damning testimonies of co-detainees and gravediggers in a recent report (co-authored with Jammu Kashmir Coalition of Civil Society, or JKCCS) to demonstrate that the cycle of illegal detentions, torture and deaths still continues.[218] APDP is the oldest human rights group in the state and led to the formation of JKCCS, a federation of human rights organizations, in 2000. The two organizations remain the bulwarks of the campaign for human rights in the region.

In January 2020, the protest at Shaheen Bagh, became the focal point of the anti-CAA-NRC campaign and inspired more such sit-ins in different parts of the country. A protest that was peaceful and fronted by women, giving it an almost moral high ground. People of different religions started congregating at Shaheen Bagh. A group of Sikhs started a langar, a library was set up and a map of India was pitched with the message, '*Hum bharat ke log CAA-NPR-NRC nahi maante*' (We, the people of India, say no to CAA-NPR-NRC).[219]

The National Population Register (NPR) is defined as the 'register of usual citizens of the country'. The census website elaborates: 'A usual resident is defined for the purposes of NPR as a person who has resided in a local area for the past six months or more, or a person who intends to reside in that area for the next six months or more.' It was first prepared with data collected in the census survey of 2010, conducted under the then Congress government. It was due to be updated in the census survey of 2021. But protestors feared that this would become the basis of NRC and be used to possibly disenfranchise Muslims. The government rejected these fears with senior ministers clarifying that NPR and NRC were not linked, prompting news outlets to dig out earlier contradictory statements.[220] And the cycle of anxiety and denial continued.

For Duaa, it could seem like a mouthful of acronyms. She had lived without the internet for more than five months, and this battle was distant. For Kashmiri Muslims, a people that already felt deeply disenfranchised, there might not have been any more fear to be felt or energy left for taking on a new rebellion. That, too, a fight, ironically, for safeguarding the

The role of the police was questioned throughout the citizenship law demonstrations. Critics saw it as pushing the government's agenda by quelling democratic dissent by force. For a people who were feeling disenfranchised, despite the government's assertion to the contrary, needed engagement, not pushbacks that can build resentment and anger, susceptible to a slight provocation.

Delhi
26 January 2020

Dear Duaa,

I feel anxious as I read about the situation of the students in your letter and see my future in the same light too. That is because it seems that education is not very important for the current government. And looking at the kind of changes that are being brought into the education sector, it is hard to say where they will take us.

The statement by Niti Aayog's member, V.K. Saraswat is not a first. Many people have made statements about Kashmir, education or health earlier also. A couple of years ago, then Union Minister of State Ashwini Kumar Choubey had also said that Biharis are unnecessarily crowding Delhi's AIIMS hospital. That statement was also heartbreaking. I just want to give you an idea that it's not just Kashmir, but many states for which the government has said many things.

I feel that people here consider Kashmir a precious property of the country and don't give any importance to the people of Kashmir. Just last week, there was a discussion on the film *Shikara* on TV. It is releasing on 7 February. The film is based on Kashmiri Pandits. There has been no discussion on their plight for the past thirty years here. And I don't think that people will go to watch this film or talk about it even now. Because before that TV discussion, we hadn't even heard the name of the film.

I think whether it's Kashmir or any region in north or south of India, people living anywhere should have access to internet, education, health and have equal rights. The one thing I have learnt from this movement against CAA-NRC is that rights are not guaranteed by laws, instead to get them one has to come out on the streets.

On 26 January, security is beefed up everywhere, traffic slows down, but there is never more than one or two days of public holiday. Is it that every year, your classes are shut down a week earlier or has this happened only this time? I believe this is absolute harassment for students and hope that all of this gets all right soon, so that you and all of Kashmir's students are able to get back to their studies properly.

Remember the last time we exchanged letters and then did a live interaction through BBC, both of us got trolled heavily. But I really like our friendship, and through our letters I have been able to understand a lot about Kashmir and Muslims which is different from common perceptions. We have lots of family friends who are Muslim but are unable to discuss such issues with them openly, lest we offend them. This CAA-NRC issue motivated me to protest, even though I am a Hindu. Because I believe that discrimination against anyone is discrimination and that we need to oppose it anyhow. And I want to know from you, if in today's changing circumstances, you and your family experience any fear because of being Muslim?

As I close my letter, I want to tell you that as I have understood Kashmir through your letters, it has removed my apprehensions and made me even more curious about Kashmir and Kashmiris. Earlier I was afraid because of the image created by the society and the media, but after our conversations, I am excited to go to Kashmir to understand and experience it myself. Is the Kashmir Valley open for people from outside now?

Wishing that we stay in touch.

Saumya

Mecca
2 February 2020

Dear Saumya,

I am writing this letter not from Kashmir, but from one of the most holy cities of the world, Mecca, Saudi Arabia. Mecca is the most holy city for us Muslims. It is the city in which our last Prophet Muhammad (PBUH) was born and where he received his first sermon from Allah through Angel Gabriel in the cave of Hira or Gar-i-Hira. Being in this city, seeing Kaaba for the first time is a feeling that I can't even describe in a few words. All I can say is that it's an amazing feeling to watch Muslims from all around the world come and pray here.

In your last letter, you had asked me about fear among Muslims. I'm a Muslim from Kashmir, a conflict zone. When this new citizenship law was passed, we people were still under Section 144 and dealing with the side effects of the removal of Article 370. We people did no business, suffered huge losses after literally sitting at home for more than six months. As a result, we are not even thinking about this new act because if we do, that would mean another six months of captivity. I speak only for Kashmiri Muslims and have no information about fear faced by Muslims of other cities.

I feel glad that you now know the truth about Kashmir. The Valley is open for tourists now (officially), but for us Kashmiris it was and will always be open for the people outside. Most of the people (around 80 per cent) in Kashmir are associated with tourism so that official order released last year about tourists, not just forced tourists and the working sector from outside to flee, but it was also responsible for huge losses that people associated with tourism faced. When that order was released, it was time for Amarnath Yatra and various other yatras were also going on. Because of that order, all the yatras were suspended for the first time in Kashmir and it caused a lot of trouble to the yatris (pilgrims). You should know that Amarnath Yatra was not suspended even in the 1990s when militancy was at its peak in Kashmir.

Talking about orders, the 1990s and since you've seen the trailer of *Shikara*, you must know that there was an order released that forced the Kashmiri Pandits to leave Kashmir. To be honest, I feel it is an issue that needs to be raised at the global level. That order not just forced the Kashmiri Pandits to evacuate but also broke the brotherhood between Kashmiri Muslims and Pandits. You know there is a place in the Khanyar area of Kashmir where the worshipping places of different religions are located on one hill. At the bottom is a gurudwara, in the middle is a shrine called the Makhdoom Sahib shrine and at the top is a temple. My mother's maiden home was near that area and they had Pandits as their neighbours. In my childhood, my mother used to tell me various stories about the brotherhood between different communities in Kashmir. Most of the stories revolved around a Kashmiri Pandit lady who was their neighbour. She used to ask my grandfather to take her to the temple in the morning when he would leave for Fajr (morning prayer). My grandfather used to drop the lady at the temple, then he used to come down, offer namaz and wait for the lady to come down and they would go home together. Looking back at this story now, I realize the intensity of the brotherhood that was broken by a mere official order.

Kashmir is a really beautiful place to live and I pray to the Almighty in this holy city of Mecca to make Kashmir a peaceful place again and to restore the brotherhood that was lost.

I'm closing this letter with the hope that my dua (wish) comes true and you will come to Kashmir to meet me.

With lots of love,
Duaa

HISTORIES

On the morning of 26 January 2020, a public holiday, as Saumya started writing her last letter to Duaa, and millions of Indians sat glued to their TV screens for the live telecast of the annual Republic Day parade, they witnessed a page being turned in the republic's history. The prime minister stepped out of his car and, instead of turning towards India Gate, walked to the National War Memorial. The wreath to remember the sacrifices of the country's soldiers in defending its borders would now onwards be laid at this memorial, commissioned by his government during its first term in 2015 and inaugurated by him the previous year. It has names of soldiers who were martyred in the wars between India and Pakistan in 1947, 1965, 1971, 1999 Kargil stand-off, and with China in 1962, among others. The camera zoomed out, revealing the shape of a *chakravyuh* (an ancient circular battle formation). This new memorial had a new '*Amar Jawan Jyoti*' burning at the centre. As the prime minister walked towards it, the India Gate, with the inverted bayonet and soldier's helmet below its arch, faded in the background.

In Jammu and Kashmir, that was observing its first Republic Day as a union territory, the more things changed, the more they remained the same. The lieutenant governor G.C. Murmu, in his address on the eve of Republic Day, asked for people's support, partnership and confidence in the government that had 'been working and dreaming really big for the people of Jammu and Kashmir'.[227] He called it a 'new dawn' that promised 'hope, prosperity, progress and peace'.

But 26 January dawned as usual. Mobile internet and mobile phone services, which had been restored a day ago, were snapped,[228] as they had been on every Independence Day and Republic Day since 2005, when on 15 August a mobile phone was used by militants to trigger a blast. The Valley remained cut off from the rest of India as it celebrated its integration into the union while senior political leaders remained in detention, now for more than six months. Iltija Mufti, daughter of Mehbooba Mufti, tweeted using her mother's handle, 'The hypocrisy of Republic Day celebrations by BJP-led government that's wilfully desecrated and violated Indian Constitution isn't lost on anyone.'

There was some change. The Sher-i-Kashmir Police Medal for Gallantry and Sher-i-Kashmir Police Medal for Meritorious Service were renamed the Jammu and Kashmir medals.[229] 'Sher-i-Kashmir' is a term used to refer to Sheikh Abdullah, the leader of Kashmir who was instrumental in negotiating its special status under Article 370. Earlier, in December, Sheikh Abdullah's birth anniversary was removed from the list of official holidays for the year 2020. News outlets had reported discussions to rename many significant buildings to remove 'Sher-i-Kashmir' from their names from on.[236] This judgement was criticized by international human rights groups like Amnesty International.[237]

The Pandit exodus, though driven by Islamic militancy, raised questions about the role of the government in protecting its citizens. The former state of Jammu and Kashmir was under governor's rule when the exodus happened in January 1990. Critics have argued that the Central government encouraged the Pandits to leave as that helped in giving the conflict a communal colour.

Duaa firmly believed that the migration of Kashmiri Pandits was 'politically motivated by the then Central government and then blamed on Muslims.' It was, she said, hard to imagine that a 'whole community could just disappear overnight without any government aid' and that she and many fellow Kashmiris believed that then governor Jagmohan Malhotra encouraged it. There was never an inquiry into the circumstances leading to the exodus of Pandits, so all that is left is speculation.

What many Pandits had hoped would be a brief departure, has stretched on for three decades. Many accounts detail the mental and physical trauma of living in tents and relief camps as a 'displaced' community for many years. Many Pandits sold their houses off, while others were taken over by Muslim neighbours. Finally, in 2004, then prime minister, Manmohan Singh and then chief minister, Mufti Mohammad Sayeed made the first announcements about resettling displaced Pandits into Kashmir and initiating confidence-building measures between the communities.[238] Townships were built to replace the camps, but they remained like ghettos in different parts of the former state. According to an estimate by the Srinagar-based Sanjay Tickoo of the Kashmiri Pandit Sangharsh Samiti (Kashmiri Pandit's Struggle Committee), more than 800 Kashmiri Pandit families live in almost 300 locations in the Valley.[239] But most Pandits, over the three decades since they left, have now settled in Jammu, Delhi and different parts of India and abroad. Periodic demands for their resettlement in the Valley are made and articles written, but many argue that the desire to return is more for the longing of the lost Kashmiri tehzeeb and identity, not with an intent to live or settle down in Kashmir.

The Valley has changed, generations have grown up and died, and there aren't that many employment opportunities. But some of the Pandit community mourns for the loss of the syncretic culture and yearns for justice and accountability. Film-maker Anmol Tikoo, a Kashmiri Pandit, argues that a true possibility of resettlement or rebuilding can only take place only if both communities get justice for the losses and grief they have suffered, 'A Kashmir where Kashmiri Pandits have full democratic and human rights, where they live as citizens without fear, can only be a Kashmir where everyone has these rights.'[240]

The exodus of the Kashmiri Pandits is a painful part of Kashmir's history, Duaa agrees, but insists that her present is different. Later she would tell me about her best friend, who is a non-Muslim, and their mutual respect for each other's religions. That, sometimes, when 'azan is going on, she covers her head' and that Duaa had 'been to a gurudwara and had the langar.' She would share an incident to press her point. At a school camp, when they were discussing each other's religions, her friend said she loved listening to *qirat* (the way Quran is recited), to which she started playing her one of the best-known verses of Quran, 'Ayat Al Kursi' on YouTube. Duaa said, 'She didn't have anything to cover her head at that time, so she went and put a blanket on her head to cover herself.'

The exodus of Kashmiri Pandits and the destruction of the Babri Masjid are underscored by some historians as two defining moments in the course of communalization in India.[241] While the latter remained a centre point, defining India's politics and the country's trajectory, the former has appeared more as a footnote, almost an afterthought.

Incidentally, even in the two letter exchanges between Saumya and Duaa, it makes an appearance now, towards the end.

In her first letter itself, Saumya's question about demographics reveals the absence of the Kashmiri Hindu in a young person's popular imagination:

> *Here, whenever people hear anything about Kashmir, the one word that comes to their mind is 'Muslim'. I want to know if it's true that only Muslims live there?*

Duaa clarifies that that is not the case and emphasizes that her lived reality is of Hindu-Muslim amity:

> *All the people here in Kashmir live with a strong brotherhood bond irrespective of their religion. We all believe in an Urdu phrase meaning all the Muslims, Hindus, Sikhs, Christians are brothers.*

But in Saumya's world, Kashmir largely remained the story between Kashmiri Muslims, the Indian state and the call for freedom. The curiosity about Kashmiri Pandits introduced only with the forthcoming release of a Bollywood film, *Shikara* (2020), one of two films based on the exodus, the other being *Sheen* (2004). Both films made by individuals directly linked to the community. *Shikara* was directed by Vidhu Vinod Chopra, whose mother was a Kashmiri Pandit and *Sheen* by Ashoke Pandit, himself a Kashmiri Pandit.

Popular cinema has been the bridge between the country and Kashmir. A region that mesmerizes, intrigues and becomes a playground for patriotism, nationalism and machismo. It began with films like *Junglee* (1961), *Kashmir Ki Kali* (1964), *Kabhie Kabhie* (1976) and *Noorie* (1979) that used the Valley as a pretty backdrop, the breathtaking beauty becoming the preferred scenery of Bollywood.

The snow-peaked mountains, vast green valleys, fiery chinar trees, tulip and rose-lined gardens, shikaras on serene lakes, women donning the local attire, all peppered in the romantic storylines set in the 'paradise on Earth'.

Once insurgency took root, the popular narrative in cinema shifted to violence within a scenic setting. The Kashmiri Muslim motivated by religion, persuaded to use violence as his means, and the Indian consumed with patriotism to defend his country and Kashmir. Masculine depictions of villains and heroes, humanized by the token women protagonists Like *Roja* (1992), with its popular scene of the Indian jumping over a burning flag to douse the flames while the Kashmiri Muslim fights the Indian state. Or *Mission Kashmir* (2000), where the trailer itself makes the juxtaposition clear by pitting 'one man consumed by rage' against 'one man bound by duty'.[242] *Yahaan* (2005), the story of a local Kashmiri woman and a Hindu Indian officer also portrays the Kashmiri Muslim brother taking up the separatist cause. The wife, sister, lover repeatedly trying to rescue the indoctrinated men from themselves.

But as writers and researchers who have engaged deeply have found, Kashmir was not the simple story of the locals caught in the crossfire between security forces and militants. Arundhati Roy wrote in one of her essays on Kashmir, of a web of informers, extortionists, intelligence agencies, and money, weapons, power at play in the Valley and that 'there are not always clear lines that demarcate the boundaries between all the things and people'.[243]

In Bollywood, the last decade offered some different portrayals of Kashmir and its Muslims, men and women. *Lamhaa* (2010) tried to capture the various stakeholders that benefit from keeping the Kashmir issue alive through the story of an Indian intelligence officer, a former militant and a separatist leader's daughter. *Raazi* (2018) had a Kashmiri Muslim woman as the protagonist following her father's footsteps to become a spy for her country, placing patriotism above all else. But it was *Haider* (2014), directed by Vishal Bhardwaj, who co-wrote the screenplay with Kashmiri author, Basharat Peer, which won critical acclaim for a brave telling of the struggle in the Valley and its questioning of the strategies adopted by the government and security forces.[244] *Haider*, set in the 1990s, followed the journey of a young Kashmiri Muslim to trace his 'disappeared' father. The screenplay tied many competing interests in the Valley, from the role of '*Ikhwanis*' (the counter insurgency group of surrendered militants, who later collaborated with the armed forces) and fake encounters to half-widows and media reporting, while also bringing a note of cynicism on the cycle of revenge and violence. And the film came with a strong recommendation from Duaa in the last letter she wrote to Saumya when they first exchanged letters in 2017.

> *I know it must sound quite confusing, but if you want to understand what Kashmiris want freedom from, then I highly recommend you to watch the Bollywood movie Haider. Everything in that movie about Kashmir is true. Everything but the English accent of the people.*

The letters had been a dialogue. A slow probing conversation. Made richer with the openness of minds and the deliberation that distance and time induced. Uncomfortable questions that had remained unsaid, found the confidence to be expressed, as pen was put on paper. Saumya asked about stone pelting girls, chants of 'Azadi' and the fear of being Muslim:

> *We have lots of family friends who are Muslim but are unable to discuss such issues with them openly, lest we offend them. This CAA–NRC issue motivated me to protest, even though I am a Hindu. Because I believe that discrimination against anyone is discrimination and that we need to oppose it anyhow. And I want to know from you, if in today's changing circumstances, you and your family experience any fear because of being Muslim?*

It had also removed fear. Perhaps, a smokescreen had lifted, of fears, myths, perceptions that Saumya attributed to the society and media. She wasn't apprehensive anymore, but curious. She had never been to Kashmir, didn't know anyone there. Now when she had made a friend, was the Valley open? She asked in her last letter in 2020, could she visit Kashmir to experience it for herself?

Duaa didn't write her reply to that last letter from Srinagar. Her family had made plans to go on a pilgrimage to Mecca and she took a flight soon after receiving Saumya's last letter. I, too, boarded a flight to come back to Delhi after five months in London. It felt strange to be in my country, in Delhi, yet still very far from Duaa. There should have been uncertainty about contacting her and getting that last leg of the conversation completed, as now I did not have the help of a colleague to physically pick up her letter and she did not have a functioning phone number while abroad that I could reach her on.

Instead, there was confidence. As after almost six months, now in another country, she had internet on her phone. Her last letter, written on paper, was sent to me from Mecca as pictures, via her favourite social media platform, Instagram. The closing lines, a *khwahish* (hope) for *aman* (peace) and *dosti* (friendship).

> *Kashmir is a really beautiful place to live and I pray to the Almighty in this holy city of Mecca to make Kashmir a peaceful place again and to restore the brotherhood that was lost. I'm closing this letter with the hope that my dua (wish) comes true and you will come to Kashmir to meet me.*

POSTSCRIPT

And then life came to a screeching halt. A little over a month after Duaa returned to Srinagar from Mecca and I was back in Delhi from London, India went into a sudden and, what would turn out to be, one of the world's longest and strictest lockdowns. Flights, trains and all public transport suspended. Our world and lives shrank into the safety of our homes. Delhi, Srinagar. Saumya, Duaa and me. A strange kind of unity in fear, boredom and fatigue. Made stranger because we had been able to meet just before everything closed down. Like a last hurrah!

In February 2020, after the final letters were exchanged, and before the Covid lockdown, we decided to film with Saumya and Duaa. Kashif, who had shot with them back in 2017, would record this video blog of the young women reading what they had written.[245] We shot with Saumya inside her library and at the iconic India Gate in Delhi. Then we flew to Srinagar. It had to be a very short trip as Delhi was still witnessing protests against CAA-NRC and we needed to be back to report on them. Kashmir was under its own communication clampdown, the one put in place after its special status was removed. When we landed, an SMS flashed on our mobiles: 'Dear customer, as per the government instructions, the internet services have been temporarily stopped in your area.' Life slowed down. My phone lay inert. There were no notifications.

Her city's scenery was beautiful, just the way Duaa had described in her letters, far from the dirty grey pollution-marked skyline of Delhi. We gulped the clean, crisp air and ogled at the majestic mountains rising from the midst of white clouds against a clear blue sky. The winter chill was piercing and as the sun went down, the warm heat of the afternoon dissipated.

We drove down to Duaa's home. Past the serene Dal Lake, idle shikaras parked in a neat row. It was a special day for her. She had gone back to school for the first time in almost seven months. Her mother had just served us our first cup of kehwa when a beaming Duaa returned home with her father. We hugged each other. It was a meeting that had waited too long.

Just as it was reconnecting with them on the phone, meeting Duaa's family in person also had a strange comforting familiarity. We only spent a little over a day with them, filming Duaa against snow-clad peaks and inside their warm home. Her magenta-black scarf standing stark against the sky and her brown pheran blending in the warm upholstery in her *baithak*. When we were about to leave, it was as if a close relative was saying goodbye. Duaa's mother walked up to me and insisted that I take the scarf and pheran with me. It will remind you of us, she said, long after this project is over.

It wasn't the best time for a journalist to be away from Delhi. Riots had broken out between supporters and opponents of the citizenship law. There was no internet for the residents of the Valley at that time, but through our journalist networks, news had trickled to us.[246] Dozens had been killed, hundreds displaced and there were reports of widespread arson. The country's capital had not witnessed such violence since the anti-Sikh riots in 1984. Both Hindus and Muslims were impacted, but the brunt was borne largely by the Muslim community. After three days, the violence was brought under control. By then, more than fifty people had been killed.

The reasons that led to the riots have not been conclusively established. In August, a fact-finding report by the Delhi Minorities Commission concluded that speeches and statements by BJP leaders inflamed passions and led to the rioting.[247] Such as one by a BJP minister in the Central government saying traitors of the country should be shot: '*Desh ke gaddaron ko, goli maaro ***** ko.*' When I posed this to the minorities minister, Mukhtar Abbas Naqvi, he agreed that the comments by BJP leaders were wrong, but refused to divulge what action the party took against them.[248] The report also raised questions about the role of the police in responding to distress calls and in their refusal to register complaints made by Muslims, a charge the police denied. Many people were arrested, including young activists and students. When the police filed its chargesheet, it named them as the main conspirators in the 'pre-planned' violence.[249]

The arrests of young activists struck a chord among some youth. Saumya had started becoming active and vocal on social media. She would read protest poetry, post her videos and comment on various burning issues—ranging from the use of stringent laws like the Unlawful Activities (Prevention) Act (UAPA) to arrest students, suppression of dissent, the impact of climate change, to the plight of migrant workers, who lost work after the sudden announcement of the Covid lockdown and many of whom had to walk hundreds of kilometres back to their hometowns. She even became part of 'Love Azad', 'a campaign primarily launched to expose the lies of "Love Jihad" and to assert women's right to be in love and to choose her partner freely', explained her Facebook post.

'Love Jihad' is a term made popular by right-wing Hindu groups to allude to an alleged conspiracy by Muslim men to convert Hindu women into adopting Islam by marriage. It had been part of election campaign rhetoric, but started gaining traction when BJP-ruled states like Uttar Pradesh, Uttarakhand, Madhya Pradesh and Gujarat passed laws criminalizing interfaith marriages done with the motive of conversion.[250] Ministers of other BJP-ruled states like Karnataka, Assam and Haryana have spoken of their intent to bring in similar legislation. The new laws led to a spate of arrests, many of whom turned out to be based on rumours and misinformation.[251] This prompted allegations that the laws, which are non-bailable and carry jail terms of up to ten years, were being used to harass Muslim men.[252] Saumya wrote that 'in these turbulent times when love is being communalized, threatened and spaces of free expression of love are shrinking and are under scanner, they had launched this campaign to expose the nefarious designs to threaten love through lies and fabricated hate campaigns.' The term 'Love Jihad' is still not recognized in law. The Central or state governments have not been able to provide any evidence of 'Love Jihad' including to questions asked in Parliament and via applications under the Right to Information Act.[253]

Another issue Saumya would write passionately about was the 'discriminatory' nature of online exams. As she explained on a phone call to me, many students left for their hometowns because of the pandemic-related restrictions. They did not have laptops and smartphones with reliable internet connections there, which made giving exams online a very stressful and difficult experience. Saumya felt very strongly about all minorities—poor, dalit, tribal, women—and their unequal access to resources that could hamper their academic performance that year. Her own experience of giving exams online turned out to be 'horrible', she would later tell me.

But online exams and classes were an inevitable fallout of the Covid pandemic. For Duaa, it was a bittersweet experience. When I had met her, she was looking forward to normalcy returning to the Valley and her going back to school. In the seven months since the abrogation, there had been no internet and no education for most children. Unfortunately, the few days in February–March 2020, when she did go to school, was only a brief interlude as the entire country went into a lockdown soon after. The difference this time was that access to 2G network was restored in the Valley. Duaa told me it was still a 'headache' to deal with the slow speed, and video calling features couldn't be used at all, but it was better than nothing. In fact, it was a prized opportunity. Her teachers were being very creative, she explained. They used a combination of four different apps to share study material along with dozens of WhatsApp groups. At times they even put it out as public posts on their social media handles. It was the spirit of jugaad or finding fixes, she said.

Then the one-year anniversary of the abrogation came. Two days ahead of it, the Valley was put under curfew.[254] Reports claimed that this was based on intelligence inputs about violent protests planned to mark the day and keeping in mind the risk of Covid-19 in big gatherings. Outside it, in Ayodhya, a three-decade-old promise made by the BJP was being fulfilled. On 5 August 2020, the Indian prime minister laid the foundation stone to build a new temple for Lord Rama at the location where Babri Masjid had stood, before it was demolished by a mob in 1992.[255] The day was chosen, even in the midst of a pandemic, because it was auspicious, beamed the news tickers on many channels. Uttar Pradesh had reported 1,00,000 deaths due to Covid-19 by then.

For Duaa, the pandemic meant that she continued to live a relatively isolated life. Though with internet, she found it easier to stay in touch with Saumya. In one chat she told her, that deep down, Kashmiris are a bit satisfied because now the world knows how it feels. To me, she wrote about the widespread national conversation about depression and anxiety among children as they stayed at home for a long period during the pandemic. And said that that was a common experience for her and the generations before her as they were put under restrictions ever so often.

The Valley's internet shutdown has been India's longest ever. According to Software Freedom Law Centre that tracks communication shutdowns in the country, the one imposed in Kashmir ended only after 213 days with the resumption of 2G services.[256] This restoration came after the Supreme Court ruled that internet services could not be suspended indefinitely while ruling on a bunch of petitions, including one filed by journalist Anuradha Bhasin highlighting restrictions on journalists.[257] Justice N.V. Ramana, later sworn in as the chief justice of India in April 2021, while reading the judgement, spoke 'on the need to balance liberty and freedom with the issue of security'.[258] It would take almost another year for 4G to be restored in the Valley, and for other freedoms.

More than 7000 people had been taken into preventive detention after the removal of Jammu and Kashmir's special status. The minister of state for home affairs, G. Krishna Reddy revealed these numbers in response to a question in the Parliament. He stated that these included 'stone pelters, miscreants, overground workers (OGWs), separatists, etc.'[259] As a result, the Jammu and Kashmir High Court was inundated with hundreds of habeas corpus petitions.[260] The provision of filing these petitions is meant to safeguard the rights and liberties of a detained person as the court hearing the petition can demand that the person be produced in front of it and due process be followed in the case against them. But the petitions faced long adjournments, defeating the purpose of this safeguard. The majority remained pending for many months, prompting the Jammu and Kashmir High Court Bar Association to eventually write a representation to the Supreme Court.[261]

Several of the detentions had been made under the stringent Public Safety Act that permits detention of up to two years. Apart from those mentioned in Reddy's statement, prominent political leaders, including three former chief ministers who had been put under house arrest or held in detention centres, were also charged with the same act, albeit six months after their detention.[262] Of the three, eighty-three-year-old Farooq Abdullah of the National Conference was the first to be released in March 2020, followed by his son Omar later that month. Mehbooba Mufti, who had been the last chief minister of the state, heading the PDP's coalition with the BJP, was only released in October—after fourteen months of detention.

The arch-rivals then came together with four other political parties to form the People's Alliance for Gupkar Declaration (PAGD).[263] The Gupkar Declaration refers to the joint statement signed by all mainstream political parties, except the BJP, at Farooq Abdullah's residence on Gupkar

Road in Srinagar on 4 August 2019, a day before the special status of the state was removed. This declaration defended Article 370 and the alliance formed after the political leaders, release in October 2020 aimed to make efforts to restore it. One effort was to pursue the constitutional challenge to the abrogation.

In August 2019, within days of the Central government's announcement to remove Jammu and Kashmir's special status, more than twenty petitions (including by political parties in Kashmir, individuals and organizations) challenging its constitutionality were filed in the Supreme Court. The petitioners had argued that the decision of abrogation be stayed while the challenges were being heard so that steps regarding its implementation do not move forward. The five-judge constitution bench of the Supreme Court had allayed these fears saying, 'the Supreme Court can always turn the clock back'.[264] The last hearing of this bench took place in March 2020. Meanwhile, important changes regarding land ownership by non-residents and access to government jobs have been effected, laws passed to enable the administration of the two union territories, and local elections conducted.

Duaa had turned eighteen now. This could have been the first time she would have exercised her right to vote—in the District Development Council (DDC) elections that were held in the two union territories in November–December 2020. The local elections should have been a low-key affair, given the limited powers up for grabs, but were keenly watched and contested as they were the first electoral exercise in the region after the abrogation. The PAGD, BJP, a newly formed Apni Party, Congress and many individuals were in the fray.

Other voices like that of the APHC were silent as its leader Mirwaiz Umar Farrouq still remained under house arrest.[265] The JKLF had already been banned for five years in March 2019 before the Lok Sabha elections and the abrogation announcement, and its leader Yasin Malik arrested.[266] He is now facing charges of conspiracy to kidnap Rubaiya Sayeed in December 1989 and for a fatal attack on Indian air force officers in 1990.[267] The religious party, Jamaat-i-Islami was also banned for five years in that March crackdown and its leaders imprisoned.[268] A year later in May 2020, Indian security forces killed Hizbul Mujahideen commander, Riyaz Naikoo. This encounter of the thirty-five-year-old commander, most wanted since the killing of Burhan Wani, was regarded as a huge success. Reports detailed Naikoo's journey: his birth in Kashmir, career as a maths teacher and entry into HM after detention by police.[269] He was also said to have used social media to recruit youth into militancy.

The DDC elections did not see any violence, a fact that the lieutenant governor of Jammu and Kashmir highlighted in his Republic Day speech in January 2021.[270] But journalists who visited the region under a 'tightly controlled government-organized trip' reported that the place was 'still struggling under heavy-handed rule'.[271] Some other things hadn't changed much. Voter turnout and electoral outcomes remained divided on religious lines.[272] In the Muslim-dominated Kashmir Valley, 34 per cent electors turned up to vote while in the Hindu-dominated Jammu region, the turnout was about 68 per cent. Similarly, PAGD's wins were concentrated in entirely Muslim districts with barely any in the entirely Hindu districts and vice versa for the BJP. Both parties hailed the results as a victory; PAGD for winning the maximum number of seats and BJP for emerging as the single largest party.

Duaa did not vote. She said she was busy preparing for her Class XII exams at that time and she heard that not many turned up from her area for the voting anyway. I remember being very excited about going inside a polling booth, showing my ID, casting my first vote and getting my index finger inked like a badge of honour. But Duaa merely said, 'Well, Kashmir is a very different place than Delhi and elections hold a totally different meaning.' Instead, it was a driving license, she said she was most looking forward to after turning eighteen. The eighteenth year of her life though would be the pandemic year and the driving license was still a dream waiting to be realized when I last checked with her soon after she turned nineteen.

The pandemic has disrupted quite a few plans. Duaa completed Class XII while at home. There was no farewell, no special notes written for teachers and friends. It has also meant that there is a fair bit of anxiety about leaving home now. She is preparing for engineering entrance exams and despite some prestigious universities and institutes outside the Valley, she is not sure she would go there. She told me that her mother says one's own home is really one's own: '*Apna ghar apna hi ghar hota hai.*' Some of her cousins studying abroad had a really tough time with lockdowns being imposed. And even within India, the experience wasn't encouraging. Duaa spoke about instances where Kashmiri students were asked to leave their hostels overnight. It was this bullying and harassment of Kashmiri children that worried her parents.

She still feels brave enough to venture out, though there is a note of pain in that assertion. Duaa said she had interacted with a lot of people outside Kashmir and some were really welcoming and curious to know about the on ground situation, but there were also people who she felt were afraid of them. 'They think all Kashmiris are terrorists,' she said. And they believe anything that the media shows or lands into their phone in unverified messages forwarded via apps like WhatsApp.

Saumya said to me once that she felt privileged to be Duaa's friend. It was like a window to a world out of her reach. More than four years since they first started writing to each other, she has still not been able to travel to Kashmir but feels she knows it and its people so much better now. 'I think this experience has changed me a lot as a person, and impacted my perspective on Kashmir profoundly,' she said. Their continuing conversations are still a study of each other's lives. Duaa recently gave her a research project on the Kunan-Poshpora incident and Saumya shared her insights into the ongoing farmer agitation after participating in a few citizens protests for it in Delhi.[273]

They still write emails to each other, though a bit infrequently. Duaa is not a big fan of typing and sharing personal letters via the impersonal mode of emails. She would rather write them on a piece of paper, scan it and email the photo so the words retain some warmth and authenticity, just as she had done during the letter exchange project. Typed emails feel like a formal mode of communication, more suitable for writing a letter to a boss or a teacher, she told me. For her friends, they mostly chat on social media apps. Except for Saumya who convinced her to keep to emails—a small give for a special friend.

For Saumya, the project made her a letter writer. Now everyone, including her parents who live with her, write her letters for special occasions and to share special conversations. On her nineteenth birthday, all close friends and family wrote her a letter on email, she told me. Some friends do tease her, saying she lives in the era of pigeons, but then humour her by giving in to her request for writing emails or handwritten notes. 'I like the waiting and anticipation, just as I did for Duaa's replies; it is so much more special than our messages on social media apps,' she told me. There is a connection, she said, like the one with Duaa. One that has grown stronger despite meeting only once in so many years and having lived through a period when divides have only grown sharper. And it's a friendship that is taking a life of its own, spreading its wings, building bridges. Duaa has become very popular among Saumya's friends. Often their conversations begin with Duaa and her life: '*Woh teri Kashmir wali dost kaisi hai?*'

APPENDIX

KASHMIR AND INDIA—A CHRONOLOGY

1932: Sheikh Abdullah forms All Jammu and Kashmir Muslim Conference. Changes name to Jammu and Kashmir National Conference in 1939 to reflect secular ideals

1947: The Boundaries Commission awards all of Jammu and Kashmir to India. Maharaja Hari Singh signs a standstill agreement, which allows the State to maintain free movement of goods and people across borders with Pakistan too

1947: Muslim tribesmen from Pakistan attack Kashmir. Maharaja asks Indian army for help and signs instrument of accession with India. The instrument of accession retains a clause for holding a plebiscite to find out the will of the people of Jammu and Kashmir when the situation permits

1948: Sheikh Abdullah becomes prime minister of Jammu and Kashmir with the support of Indian prime minister Jawaharlal Nehru

1949: Prem Nath Dogra forms Praja Parishad to represent the interests of Jammu Hindus

1952: Delhi Agreement signed between prime minister of Jammu and Kashmir, Sheikh Abdullah and prime minister of India, Jawaharlal Nehru that gave more autonomy to the State

1952–53: Praja Parishad leads agitation opposing special status to Jammu and Kashmir, including the provision of Article 370, with the slogan, *'Ek desh main do vidhaan, do pradhan, do nishan—nahi chalenge, nahi chalenge'* (One country cannot have two Constitutions, two heads of state and two flags).

1953: Dr Syama Prasad Mukherjee, founder-president of the Bharatiya Jan Sangh, gives a national voice to Praja Parishad's demands. Takes his 'satyagraha' to Kashmir, is arrested, and dies soon after in prison

1953: Sheikh Abdullah is dismissed as prime minister of Jammu and Kashmir by Sadr-i-Riyasat Karan Singh and arrested on charges of anti-national activity after rumours emerge that he is making efforts for Kashmir's independence

1954: Delhi Agreement is adopted under the Constitution (Application to Jammu and Kashmir) Order, 1954 that specifies the terms under Article 370 and Article 35A ensuring special status to Jammu and Kashmir within India

1955: Senior National Conference leader, Mirza Afzal Beg, forms the Plebiscite Front Party to campaign for a United Nations' monitored plebiscite

1962: China defeats India in a war and gains control of Aksai Chin in eastern Kashmir

1964: Sheikh Abdullah is released briefly by the efforts of Indian prime minister Nehru, paving the way for renewed negotiations on Kashmir's status. But those are halted by Nehru's sudden death. Abdullah is imprisoned again in 1965 by then prime minister Lal Bahadur Shastri

1964: Praja Parishad merges into Bharatiya Jan Sangh (BJS) after Prem Nath Dogra is elected President of BJS

1965: A brief war between India and Pakistan results in both staying at same ceasefire positions in Kashmir

1960s: The Jammu and Kashmir Liberation Front (JKLF) is formed to campaign for an independent state of Jammu and Kashmir where Hindus and Muslims would have equal rights

1971: India defeats Pakistan in a war that helps create Bangladesh as a separate country and draws a ceasefire line between India and Pakistan in Kashmir

1972: India and Pakistan sign the Simla Agreement that delineates the Line of Control (LoC) from the ceasefire line and agree to refrain from the threat or the use of force in violation of this line

1975: Sheikh Abdullah returns to power as chief minister of Jammu and Kashmir. Signs the Kashmir Accord that gives up the demand of a plebiscite, in lieu of the people being given the right to self-rule by a democratically elected government as envisaged under Article 370

1975: Congress prime minister Indira Gandhi imposes Emergency in the country. Elections are suspended, political leaders imprisoned and the press censored

1977: Bharatiya Jan Sangh merges into Janata Party

1977: Congress party loses power in Centre for the first time since independence. Alliance of opposition parties and Janata Party form government

1977: Elections in Jammu and Kashmir, considered widely to be the first that are free and fair, take place. Sheikh Abdullah's National Conference gets a comfortable majority, Janata Party wins its first seats

1980: Former Bharatiya Jan Sangh members leave Janata Party to form Bharatiya Janata Party (BJP)

1982: Sheikh Abdullah dies and his son Farooq Abdullah succeeds as chief minister of Jammu and Kashmir

1987: Jammu and Kashmir state assembly elections are held amidst blatant rigging. The National Conference-Congress coalition's win is questioned by the Muslim United Front (MUF), a group of Islamic Kashmiri political parties

1989–90: Armed rebellion against Indian rule begins in Kashmir with a rise of Pakistan-backed militant groups in the Valley. Indian army assisted by the two paramilitary forces, the Border Security Force (BSF) and the Central Reserve police Force (CRPF) is deployed, given special powers and immunity to fight insurgency

1989: Hizbul Mujahideen, militant arm of the Jamaat-e-Islami Party emerges and campaigns for a religious pro-Pakistan rule for Kashmir

1989: Daughter of the country's then home minister Mufti Mohammad Sayeed, Rubaiya Sayeed, is kidnapped to negotiate the release of five

JKLF members. The militants are released. Hizbul Mujahideen and JKLF emerge as the two prominent separatist groups of the thirty-two operating in the Valley

1989: BJP joins the Ram Janmabhoomi movement started by the Vishva Hindu Parishad, registers a huge surge from two seats in the 1984 to 85 seats in that year's parliamentary elections.

1989: Vice president of the Jammu and Kashmir State BJP, Tika Lal Taploo is killed, followed by murders of other party leaders

1990: BJP president L.K. Advani organizes a 10,000 km 'Rath Yatra' to further mobilize support of Hindus

1990: Fearing attacks by militants, thousands of Kashmiri Pandits start fleeing the Valley. The largest exodus takes place in the month of January 1990. The government is accused of not being able to protect the community

1991–92: BJP president Murali Manohar Joshi leads 'Ekta Yatra' beginning from Kanyakumari to conclude in Kashmir. Joshi is able to hoist the Indian flag in the army fortified Lal Chowk in Srinagar amidst threats of militant attacks and a strict curfew

1992: The Babri Masjid is broken by a violent Hindu mob triggering communal riots. Retaliation and attacks across the country kill hundreds

1993: All Parties Hurriyat Conference, an amalgamation of twenty-six religious and political parties, is formed to campaign peacefully for Kashmir's self-rule

1994: Association of Parents of Disappeared Persons (APDP) is founded by Parveena Ahangar to campaign and demand for information about 'enforced disappearances' in Kashmir

1996: BJP forms its first government in the country, though it falls within thirteen days. After a crackdown on militancy, Parliamentary elections are able to be held in Jammu and Kashmir too. BJP registers its first victory by winning the Udhampur Lok Sabha seat

1999: Congress leader Mufti Mohammad Sayeed leaves to form his own regional party, the Peoples Democratic Party (PDP) with the promise of self-rule for the state of Jammu and Kashmir

1999: India and Pakistan come head-to-head in a war as militants cross into Kargil district

1999: BJP-led National Democratic Alliance (NDA) forms government in the Centre that goes on to complete a full term

2004: Prime minister Manmohan Singh and chief minister of Jammu and Kashmir, Mufti Mohammad Sayeed make the first announcements about resettling displaced Kashmiri Pandits back into Kashmir and initiating confidence-building measures between Hindu-Muslim communities

2008: Protests erupt after a controversy over the transfer of forest land to the organizers of the Hindu pilgrimage, the Amarnath Yatra. Sixty people die and a 1000 are injured in the two-month long agitation. The order is reversed by the government

2009: Another summer of violent protests after allegations of rape and murder of two women by Indian security forces. Eighty people are injured as questions are raised on the investigation and a public inquiry commission instituted

2010: More than 100 people, mostly youth, die in protests and clashes after a seventeen-year-old, Tufail Mattoo, is killed by a tear gas shell fired by security forces deployed at an anti-India demonstration

2013: Group of fifty young women renew the legal battle in the 1991 Kunan–Poshpora case of alleged mass rape by a regiment of the Indian army on the women of the twin villages. Army denies all allegations

2014: NDA registers the biggest victory in Parliamentary elections in three decades. Narendra Modi is sworn in as the prime minister

2014: BJP registers their best ever electoral success in the Jammu and Kashmir state assembly elections

2015: After months of intense negotiations, BJP and PDP form a coalition with Mufti Mohammad Sayeed as chief minister. BJP is in power in the state for the first time ever. After Mufti Mohammad Sayeed's death in 2016, his daughter Mehbooba Mufti is sworn in as the chief minister

2016: Student leaders Kanhaiya Kumar, Umar Khalid and others arrested for raising anti-India slogans in a Kashmir-related protest at Jawaharlal Nehru University

2016: Young popular militant leader and top commander of the Hizbul Mujahideen group, Burhan Wani, is killed in an encounter. Worst unrest since the 1990s engulfs the Valley. An estimated 100 to 380 people die and thousands injured as stone pelters clash with security forces that use pellet guns

2016: In the interest of maintenance of public order, the government imposes month-long ban blocking access to twenty-two social networking sites, including WhatsApp, Facebook, Twitter and Telegram

2016: Militants attack the Indian army's brigade headquarters near Uri, killing nineteen soldiers

2016: Indian army crosses the LoC and launches what it terms as a 'surgical strike' in Pakistan-administered Kashmir. India claims it hit 'terror launch pads', which Pakistan denies

2017: Srinagar parliamentary constituency by-election witnesses the lowest ever turnout. Polling day is marred by looting of EVMs and vandalism at polling booths. Eight civilians are killed and 170 injured

2017: Videos surface on social media showing intimidation of security forces by some youth. Another video of a civilian, Farooq Dar, tied to a jeep by the Indian army to use as human shield against stone pelters becomes viral, provoking large-scale protests

2018: An eight-year-old girl from the Muslim nomadic tribe of Bakkarwals is raped and murdered. Investigators arrest some Hindu men for the crime. Case acquires religious colour after two BJP legislators participate in a rally in support of the accused. They are eventually forced to resign after outrage across the country. Six of seven accused are convicted in 2019

2018: BJP withdraws support to PDP citing 'national security and integrity' and the coalition government falls

2019: Forty CRPF jawans are killed in a suicide attack on the Srinagar–Jammu national highway in Pulwama. Jaish-e-Mohammad (JeM) takes responsibility, releases video of the suicide bomber, a young Kashmiri man, Adil Ahmed Dar

2019: Indian air force crosses into Pakistan's territory to target the biggest training camps of JeM in Balakot. India claims this second 'surgical strike' eliminated large number of JeM terrorists. Pakistan denies this and declares it has carried out its own strikes from its own airspace the next day, downing two Indian aircrafts and capturing one pilot. Wing Commander Abhinandan Varthaman is released in a couple of days as a 'peace gesture' by Pakistan

2019: Narendra Modi creates history by becoming the only non-Congress prime minister to retain power for a second term with full majority. BJP-led NDA becomes the only non-Congress government to return to power after a full term in the Parliament

2019: There is a massive build-up of troops in Jammu and Kashmir, the Amarnath Yatra is stopped and tourists airlifted. All political leaders are placed under house arrest. Landline, mobile and internet services blocked overnight. The Parliament is informed by the home minister that the special status enjoyed by the state of Jammu and Kashmir under Article 370 and 35A has been removed under 'The Constitution (Application to Jammu and Kashmir) Order, 2019' and the state reorganized into two union territories, Jammu and Kashmir and Ladakh

2019: Citizenship Amendment Act (CAA) is passed by both Houses of Parliament. Protests erupt across the country claiming the law is anti-Muslim and harms the secular fabric of India. At least twenty people die and hundreds are injured as they turn confrontational and police uses violent force to disperse protestors

2020: An armed mob of about fifty masked people attacks teachers and students in Jawaharlal Nehru University, breaking glass windows and furniture. Thirty people are injured

2020: Delhi witnesses the worst riots since 1983 when more than fifty people are killed in clashes between supporters and opponents of the citizenship law

2020: Foundation stone for a Rama temple is laid by prime minister Modi in Ayodhya where the Babri mosque stood

2020: District Development Council elections are held in the two newly formed union territories of Jammu and Kashmir and Ladakh

ENDNOTES

Pen on Paper

[1] Lydia Polgreen, 'Youth's Death in Kashmir Renews a Familiar Pattern of Crisis', *The New York Times*, 11 July 2010, https://www.nytimes.com/2010/07/12/world/asia/12kashmir.html

[2] Amit Baruah, 'Why Kashmir is again on a knife edge', *BBC News*, 10 August 2010, https://www.bbc.com/news/world-south-asia-10925145

Asiya Jan, 17, and Neelofar Jan, 22, were allegedly raped and murdered by security forces in May 2009. At least eighty people were injured in protests that continued for a month and a half after the incident as questions were raised on the investigation and a public inquiry commission headed by Justice (Retired) Muzaffar Jan was appointed by then Jammu and Kashmir Chief Minister Omar Abdullah. For more, read Report: International People's Tribunal on Human Rights and Justice in Kashmir, 'Militarization with Impunity: A Brief on Rape and Murder in Shopian, Kashmir', *kashmirprocess.org*, 19 July 2009, https://jkccs.files.wordpress.com/2017/05/shopian-rape-and-murder-report.pdf

[3] Gowhar Geelani, *Kashmir: Rage and Reason* (New Delhi, Rupa Publications, 2019), 1–10.

[4] Shujaat Bukhari, 'Why the death of militant Burhan Wani has Kashmiris up in arms', *BBC News*, 11 July 2016, https://www.bbc.com/news/world-asia-india-36762043

[5] Sameer Yasir, 'Kashmir unrest: What was the real death toll in the state in 2016?', *FirstPost*, 2 January 2017, https://www.firstpost.com/india/kashmir-unrest-what-was-the-real-death-toll-in-the-state-in-2016–3183290.html

[6] 'Digital India: Technology to transform a connected nation', Digital India Report April 2019, McKinsey Global Institute, accessed 11th June 2020, https://www.mckinsey.com/~/media/McKinsey/Business%20Functions/McKinsey%20Digital/Our%20Insights/Digital%20India%20Technology%20to%20transform%20a%20connected%20nation/MGI-Digital-India-Report-April-2019.ashx

[7] Simon Kemp, 'India overtakes the USA to become Facebook's #1 country', *The Next Web*, 13 July 2017, https://thenextweb.com/contributors/2017/07/13/india-overtakes-usa-become-facebooks-top-country/

[8] Suresh Matthew, '"Dangal" Girl Zaira Wasim Deletes Controversial Open Letter', *The Quint*, 17 January 2017, https://www.thequint.com/entertainment/zaira-wasim-dangal-girl-meets-jammu-kashmir-chief-minister-mehbooba-mufti-writes-shocking-open-letter

Kashmir

[9] Mudasir Ahmed, 'Why the Resignation of the PDP's Srinagar MP is a Big Deal', *The Wire,* 16 September 2016, https://thewire.in/politics/cracks-pdp-begin-show-calling-party-rss-facilitator-srinagar-mp-resigns

[10] 'Srinagar Parliamentary Constituency', Chief Electoral Officer UT of Jammu Kashmir and Ladakh, accessed 11 June 2020, http://ceojammukashmir.nic.in/Parliamentary_Constituencies.htm

[11] Sonia Sarkar, 'India elections: Why are Kashmiris not voting?', *DeutcheWelle*, 30 April 2019, https://www.dw.com/en/india-elections-why-are-kashmiris-not-voting/a-48547313

[12] 'By-elections Result 2017: Jammu-Kashmir 2-Srinagar (PC)', Election Commission of India, accessed 11 June 2020, https://eci.gov.in/files/file/2602-bye-election-result-2017-jammu-kashmir-2-srinagar-pc/

[13] Peerzada Ashiq, 'Lowest ever turnout in Srinagar Lok Sabha bypoll', *The Hindu*, 9 April 2017, https://www.thehindu.com/news/national/lowest-ever-turnout-in-srinagar-bypoll/article17896913.ece

[14] 'Demographics', Jammu and Kashmir Government, accessed 12 June 2020, https://jk.gov.in/jammukashmir/?q=demographics

[15] M.J. Akbar, *Kashmir: Behind the Vale* (New Delhi: Roli Books, 2002), 97–99.

[16] Dominique Lapierre & Larry Collins, *Freedom at Midnight* (Noida: Vikas Publishing House, 1997), 434–436.

[17] Dominique Lapierre & Larry Collins, *Freedom at Midnight* (Noida: Vikas Publishing House, 1997), 317–319.

[18] Dominique Lapierre & Larry Collins, *Freedom at Midnight* (Noida: Vikas Publishing House, 1997), 541–548.

[19] Andrew Whitehead, *A Mission in Kashmir* (New Delhi: Penguin India, 2007), 108–121.

[20] M.J. Akbar, *Kashmir: Behind the Vale* (New Delhi: Roli Books, 2002), 112-113.

[21] 'J & K State having District Boundaries', Chief Electoral Officer UT of Jammu and Kashmir And UT of Ladakh, accessed 11 September 2020, http://ceojammukashmir.nic.in/JKMaps/JKNEW.pdf

[22] 'Geographical Features of Jammu and Kashmir', J & K Forest Department Government of Jammu and Kashmir, accessed 12 June 2020, http://jkforest.gov.in/geo_area.html#:~:text=Jammu

[23] 'Demographics', Jammu and Kashmir Government, accessed 12 June 2020, https://jk.gov.in/jammukashmir/?q=demographics

[24] Reuters Staff, 'Majority in Kashmir Valley want independence: poll', *Reuters*, 13 August 2007, https://www.reuters.com/article/us-kashmir-poll/majority-in-kashmir-Valley-want-independence-poll-idUSDEL29179620070813

[25] Jammu and Kashmir had its own prime minister and *Sadr-e-Riyasat* (Head of State) until 1965, when the J & K Constitution was amended (Constitution of J & K (Sixth Amendment) Act, 1965) by then Congress government, which replaced the two positions with chief minister and governor respectively.

[47] Umar Ganie (@UmarGanie1), 'Girl students kicks a police vehicle during a protest at Lal Chowk in Srinagar. Violent clashes erupt after colleges were re-opened #kashmir', Twitter photo, 24 April 2017 https://twitter.com/UmarGanie1/status/856477906112921602

[48] Anuradha Bhasin Jamwal, 'Kashmiri Women as Stone Pelters: It Is Not Just Anti-Militarism, It's About Empowerment!', *The Citizen*, 27 April 2017, https://www.thecitizen.in/index.php/en/NewsDetail/index/2/10538/Kashmiri-Women-as-Stone-Pelters-It-Is-Not-Just-Anti-Militarism-Its-About-Empowerment

[49] Fayaz Wani, 'J-K police high-handedness compelled me to pick up stones: Afshan Ashiq', *The New Indian Express*, 16 May 2017, https://www.newindianexpress.com/nation/2017/may/16/j-k-police-high-handedness-compelled-me-to-pick-up-stones-afshan-ashiq-1605236.html

[50] Avani Rai & Parshati Dutta, 'Footballer to stone pelter: What made Afshan Ashiq, the woman in blue, pick up that rock?', *Scroll*, 9 May 2017, https://scroll.in/article/837003/footballer-to-stone-pelter-what-made-afshan-ashiq-the-girl-in-blue-pick-up-that-rock

[51] Annie Gowen, 'Teen girls with stones are the new threat in India's Kashmir conflict', *Washington Post*, 29 April 2017, https://www.washingtonpost.com/world/asia_pacific/teen-girls-with-stones-are-the-new-threat-in-indias-kashmir-conflict/2017/04/28/5933168a-2a92-11e7-9081-f5405f56d3e4_story.html

[52] Essar Batool, Ifrah Butt, Samreena Mushtaq, Munaza Rashid, Natasha Rather, *Do you remember Kunan-Poshpora?* (New Delhi: Zubaan, 2016), 2–8.

[53] Sameer Yasir, 'Kashmir unrest: Following Pulwama clashes, schools and colleges stay shut for fifth day', *Firstpost*, 22 April 2017, https://www.firstpost.com/india/kashmir-unrest-following-pulwama-degree-college-clashes-schools-and-colleges-stay-shut-for-fifth-day-3398368.html

[54] Mudasir Ahmed, 'Mehbooba Mufti Once Opposed Internet Shutdown in Kashmir. Now She's Done the Same', *The Wire*, 27 April 2017, https://thewire.in/politics/kashmir-internet-ban-social-media

[55] 'Living in Digital Darkness: A Handbook on Internet Shutdowns in India', Software Freedom Law Centre, 2018, accessed 16 June

2020, https://sflc.in/living-digital-darkness-handbook-internet-shutdowns-india

Perceptions

[56] Deepak Dobhal, 'Pellet Guns Used Against Kashmir Protesters', *Voice of America*, 26 July 2016, https://www.voanews.com/episode/pellet-guns-used-against-kashmir-protesters-3726681

[57] Gafira Qadir, 'In Srinagar, "increased military gaze" after August 2019 makes women uncomfortable', *The Kashmirwallah*, 13 August 2020, https://thekashmirwalla.com/2020/08/in-srinagar-increased-military-gaze-after-august-2019-makes-women-uncomfortable/

[58] Hilal Mir, 'From symbol of conflict to objet d'art: Tracing the bunker's presence in Kashmir', *Firstpost*, 11 January 2018, https://www.firstpost.com/living/from-symbol-of-conflict-to-objet-dart-tracing-the-bunkers-presence-in-kashmir-4289857.html

[59] Ramachandra Guha, *India After Gandhi: The History of the World's Largest Democracy* (London: Pan Macmillan, 2007), 622–623.

[60] Rekha Chowdhary, 'The Vacuum of Mainstream Politics in Kashmir', *The Wire*, 30 September 2019, https://thewire.in/rights/the-vacuum-of-mainstream-politics-in-kashmir

[61] Ramachandra Guha, *India After Gandhi: The History of the World's Largest Democracy* (London: Pan Macmillan, 2007), 252–253.

[62] Shakir Mir, 'When Pro-Plebiscite Kashmiris Found Common Cause with "Hindu Nationalists"', *The Wire*, 6 May 2019, https://thewire.in/politics/when-pro-plebiscite-kashmiris-found-common-cause-with-hindu-nationalists

[63] Ramachandra Guha, *India After Gandhi: The History of the World's Largest Democracy* (London: Pan Macmillan, 2007), 349–358.

[64] Ajit Bhattacharjea, *Sheikh Mohammad Abdullah: Tragic Hero of Kashmir* (New Delhi: Roli Books, 2008), 228–231.

[65] Kul Bhushan Mahotra, *A Saga of Sacrifices: Praja Parishad Movements in Jammu and Kashmir* (Jammu: Bharatiya Janata Party, 2018), 8-11, http://library.bjp.org/jspui/handle/123456789/2687

[66] 'Jammu and Kashmir 1977', Election Commission of India, last accessed 18 June 2020, https://eci.gov.in/files/file/3791-jammu-kashmir-1977/

[67] Jamaat-e-Islami Hind, 'Our Story', Facebook, last accessed on 30 June 2020, https://www.facebook.com/JIHMarkaz/

[68] Praveen Donthi, 'How Mufti Mohammad Sayeed Shaped the 1987 Elections in Kashmir', *The Caravan*, 23 March 2016, https://caravanmagazine.in/vantage/mufti-mohammad-sayeed-shaped-1987-kashmir-elections

[69] Report by Joint Fact-finding Committee of Organizations for Democratic Rights and Civil Liberties, *Blood in the Valley: Kashmir—Behind the propaganda curtain* (Bombay: Lokshahi Hakk Sangathana, 1995), 40–60.

[70] M.B. Naqvi, *Pakistan at Knife's Edge* (New Delhi: Roli Books, 2015), chap. Historical Notes, https://books.google.co.in/books?id=okcmCA AAQBAJ&printsec=copyright&redir_esc=y#v=onepage&q=kashmir &f=false

[71] Jammu Kashmir Liberation Front is believed to be behind the hijacking of an Indian Airlines plane in 1971 and one of its co-founders Maqbool Bhat was allegedly involved in planning it. Maqbool Bhat was arrested in 1980 for the killing of a police officer and sentenced with the death penalty. In February 1984, JKLF members kidnapped the Indian Deputy High Commissioner in UK to demand Bhat's release. When that was turned down, the Commissioner was killed. Maqbool Bhat was hanged on 11 February 1984, and the day is marked as the Martyrdom Day in Kashmir even today. For more: South Asia Terrorism Portal, last accessed on 30 August 2020. https://www.satp.org/satporgtp/countries/india/states/jandk/terrorist_outfits/jammu_&_kashmir_liberation_front.htm

[72] Mudasir Ahmed, 'A Brief History of the J & K Liberation Front, Now Banned Under UAPA', *The Wire*, 23 March 2019, https://thewire.in/security/kashmir-jklf-ban-yasin-malik

[73] D. Suba Chandran, 'The Hizbul Mujahideen', *Institute of Peace and Conflict Studies*, 14 August 2000, http://www.ipcs.org/comm_select.php?articleNo=405

[74] Ramachandra Guha, *India After Gandhi: The History of the World's Largest Democracy* (London: Pan Macmillan, 2007), 650–654.

[75] Report by Joint Fact-finding Committee of Organizations for Democratic Rights and Civil Liberties, *Blood in the Valley: Kashmir—Behind the propaganda curtain* (Bombay: Lokshahi Hakk Sangathana, 1995), 69–84.

[76] TADA was allowed to lapse in 1995. According to Human Rights Watch, 'TADA led to tens of thousands of politically motivated detentions, torture, and other human rights violations. In the face of mounting opposition to the act, India's government acknowledged these abuses and consequently let TADA lapse in 1995.' Last accessed 22 June 2020. https://www.hrw.org/legacy/backgrounder/asia/india-bck1121.htm#:~:text=TADA

[77] 'India: Torture and Deaths in Custody in Jammu and Kashmir', *Amnesty International*, 31 January 1995, https://www.amnesty.org/en/documents/asa20/001/1995/en/#:~:text=India

[78] Basharat Peer, *Curfewed Night* (Delhi: Penguin Books, 2009), 50–56.

[79] Gowsia Jan, Dr. Sofiya Hassan Mir, Arif Hussain Malik, 'Women and Conflict Situation in Kashmir Post 1989: A Sociological Study of District of Anantnag', *Asian Journal of Research in Social Sciences and Humanities*, Vol. 6, No. 4, (April 2016): 361-367, https://www.researchgate.net/publication/300372111_Women_and_Conflict_Situation_in_Kashmir_Post_1989_A_Sociological_Study_of_District_Anantnag

[80] Akhila Raman, 'India's human rights record in J & K', *India Together*, November 2002, last accessed 12 September 2020, http://www.indiatogether.org/peace/kashmir/articles/indhr.htm

[81] Aliya Nazki, 'Kashmir "mass rape" survivors fight for justice', *BBC News*, 7 October 2017, https://www.bbc.com/news/world-asia-41268906

[82] Essar Batool, Ifrah Butt, Samreena Mushtaq, Munaza Rashid, Natasha Rather, *Do you remember Kunan-Poshpora?* (New Delhi: Zubaan, 2016), 38–40.

[83] Saeed ur Rehman Siddiqui, 'Wailing woes of Kashmiri women', *Kashmirnewz.com*, last accessed 19 June 2020, http://www.kashmirnewz.com/a0027.html

[84] 'Kashmir: Violence and Health—A quantitative assessment on violence, the psychosocial and general health status of the Indian Kashmiri population', Medecins Sans Frontieres, November 2006, https://www.msf.org/kashmir-violence-and-mental-health

[85] Essar Batool, Ifrah Butt, Samreena Mushtaq, Munaza Rashid, Natasha Rather, *Do you remember Kunan-Poshpora?* (New Delhi: Zubaan, 2016), 25–28.

Freedoms

[86] Arundhati Roy, 'The hanging of Afzal Guru is a stain on India's democracy', *The Guardian*, 10 February 2013, https://www.theguardian.com/commentisfree/2013/feb/10/hanging-afzal-guru-india-democracy

[87] Srijan Shukla, 'Maqbool Bhat, Kashmir's first radical separatist, hanged by Indira after diplomat's killing', *The Print*, 11 February 2020, https://theprint.in/past-forward/maqbool-bhat-kashmirs-first-radical-separatist-hanged-by-indira-after-diplomats-killing/363201/

[88] Muzamil Shah, 'I heard on radio that my son would be hanged following day: Maqbool Bhat's mother', *Greater Kashmir*, 11 February 2019, https://www.greaterkashmir.com/news/kashmir/i-heard-on-radio-that-my-son-would-be-hanged-following-day-maqbool-bhats-mother/

[89] Arundhati Roy, 'A perfect day for democracy', *The Hindu*, 10 February 2013, https://www.thehindu.com/opinion/lead/a-perfect-day-for-democracy/article4397705.ece

[90] Saurabh Trivedi, 'How death penalty proceedings have changed over the years', *The Hindu*, 14 December 2019, https://www.thehindu.com/news/cities/Delhi/hush-hush-executions-a-thing-of-the-past/article30301569.ece

[91] 'India-administered Kashmir observes strike to remember Afzal Guru', *TRT World*, 9 February 2020, https://www.trtworld.com/asia/india-administered-kashmir-observes-strike-to-remember-afzal-guru-33630

[92] Siddhartha Rai, 'JNU students clash over event against Afzal Guru hanging', *India Today*, 10 February 2016, https://www.indiatoday.in/mail-today/story/jnu-students-clash-over-event-against-afzal-guru-hanging-307958-2016-02-10

[93] Kritika Sharma Sebastian, 'Two JNU students raised objectionable slogans: report', *The Hindu*, 16 March 2016, https://www.thehindu.com/news/cities/Delhi/two-jnu-students-raised-objectionable-slogans-report/article8360300.ece

[94] NDTV, 'Arrested JNU student Kanhaiya Kumar, others attacked at Delhi court', YouTube, 17 February 2016, https://www.youtube.com/watch?v=r0l7EDoeYyM

[95] Mohamad Junaid, 'Azadi—Memoirs of a slogan', *Raiot.in*, March 6, 2016, http://www.raiot.in/azadi-when-it-travels-memoirs-of-a-slogan/

[96] 'JNU Sedition Row: Delhi Police Name Umar, Kanhaiya in Charge Sheet', *The Quint*, 15 January 2019, https://www.thequint.com/news/india/delhi-police-jnu-sedition-case-charge-sheet

[97] NDTV, 'Out of jail, Kanhaiya Kumar attacks PM Modi in speech on JNU campus', YouTube 3 March 2016, https://www.youtube.com/watch?v=8jkQhAE-j8s

[98] Manshes IIMC, 'Kanhaiya Kumar JNUSU president azadi aazadi', YouTube, 4 March 2016, https://www.youtube.com/watch?v=ilVWFgUlctQ

[99] Creative Commoners, 'Azadi (Dub Sharma)', YouTube, 11 April 2016, https://www.youtube.com/watch?v=TCRHm1pmzCI

[100] Samiha Nettikkara, 'Why an Indian "freedom" speech has become a viral remix', *BBC News*, 3 May 2016, https://www.bbc.com/news/world-asia-india-36032537

[101] Rohith Vemula's letter, 'My Birth is My Fatal Accident: Rohith Vemula's Searing Letter is an Indictment of Social Prejudices', *The Wire*, 17 January 2019, https://thewire.in/caste/rohith-vemula-letter-a-powerful-indictment-of-social-prejudices

[102] Sukanya Shantha, 'Rohith Vemula's Suicide Triggered a New Political Wave', *The Wire*, 17 January 2019, https://thewire.in/caste/rohith-vemula-suicide-triggered-a-new-political-wave

[103] PTI, 'Students hold "Freedom Parade" on Republic Day', *Hindustan Times*, 26 January 2013, https://www.hindustantimes.com/delhi/students-hold-freedom-parade-on-republic-day/story-a2M1Z0XNIWSUZCDqKO2pDJ.html

[104] Linda E. Carty and Chandra T. Mohanty, 'Mapping Transnational Feminist Engagements: Neoliberalism and the Politics of Solidarity', in *The Oxford Handbook of Transnational Feminist Movements*, ed. Rawwida Baksh-Soodeen, Wendy Harcourt (New York: Oxford University Press, 2015), 103-105.

[105] Malini Nair, 'The new shades of Feminism', *The Times of India*, 8 March 2015, https://timesofindia.indiatimes.com/home/sunday-times/deep-focus/The-new-shades-of-feminism/articleshow/46489802.cms

[106] Nirupama Dutt, '"Hum kya chahte? Azaadi!" Story of slogan raised by JNU's Kanhaiya', *Hindustan Times*, 5 March 2016, https://www.hindustantimes.com/punjab/kanhaiya-kumar-s-azadi-chant-not-a-gift-from-kashmir-separatists-but-from-feminists/story-K7GQNzhzE1Z8UFBDGVYh6J.html

[107] Sukant Deepak, 'Azaadi slogan originated from feminists', *DailyO*, 5 March 2016, https://www.dailyo.in/politics/azadi-kashmir-kanhaiya-kumar-jnu-sedition-kamla-bhasin/story/1/9389.html

[108] 'Pakistan: Proposed Reforms to Hudood Laws Fall Short', *Human Rights Watch*, 6 September 2006 https://www.hrw.org/news/2006/09/06/pakistan-proposed-reforms-hudood-laws-fall-short

[109] 'The Pakistani woman`s crusade against the system', *Dawn*, 15 April 2010, https://www.dawn.com/news/879183/the-pakistani-woman-s-crusade-against-the-system

[110] Haris Zargar, 'Kashmir's Resistance Anthem', *New Frame*, 15 October 2019, https://www.newframe.com/kashmirs-resistance-anthem/

[111] Mohamad Junaid, 'Azadi: Memoirs of a Slogan', *Raiot.in*, 6 March 2016, http://www.raiot.in/azadi-when-it-travels-memoirs-of-a-slogan/

[112] A Pew Research Centre survey conducted among 2521 respondents in India from 23 May to 23 July 2018 found that the majority said the situation in Kashmir had worsened in the past five years and the government should use more military force there than it was using now. For more (last accessed 12 September 2020): https://www.pewresearch.org/global/2019/03/25/a-sampling-of-public-opinion-in-india/

[113] According to the Economic Survey 2016-17 of the state of Jammu and Kashmir, the per capita income was Rs 65,615, well below the national average of Rs 98,000. The former state's rate of growth, as measured by Gross Domestic Product (GDP) too has consistently been lower than that of the country. According to Economic Surveys over the past thirty-five-year period, agriculture and its allied sectors contributed 51 per cent in 1980-81, 31 per cent in 1999-2000, 27 per cent in 2007-08 and about 16 per cent in 2016-17 to the former state's GDP. Handicraft, handloom and cottage industry contributed 28 per cent to the GDP in 2016-17. The services' sector's share has been more than half of the GDP since 2002-03 to 2016-17. That includes trade, hotels, transport, communications, financial services, real estate, public administration and defence. But just like agriculture and industry, the service sector is also slacking. Rate of growth ebbs and flows with the level of unrest in the Valley. This has impacted the sector with most potential in the region, tourism. It contributed just under 7 per cent to the state's GDP in 2016-17. For more: See Economic Surveys, Government of Jammu and Kashmir: Directorate of Economics & Statistics, last accessed on 22 June 2020, http://ecostatjk.nic.in/publications/publications.htm

[114] According to the Reserve Bank of India, the former state had almost negligible Foreign Direct Investment from 2000 to 2017, ranking at the bottom of the all India tally. For more: Foreign Direct Investment in India: Annual Issue 2017, 'Statement on RBI's Regional Offices (with State covered) received highest FDI Equity Inflows between Jan 2000 to Dec 2017', Department for Promotion of Industry and Internal Trade, last accessed 22 June 2020, https://dipp.gov.in/sia-newsletter/foreign-direct-investment-india-annual-issue-2017

[115] Qaiser Mohammad Ali, 'Weeping Willow: Why Kashmir's Bat-Making Industry Has Been Hit For A Six', *Outlook*, 24 February 2020, https://www.outlookindia.com/magazine/story/sports-news-weeping-willow-why-kashmirs-bat-making-industry-has-been-hit-for-a-six/302770

[116] The former state's poverty rate was found half of the country's average in Reserve Bank of India's 2012 report based on the Tendulkar Poverty line. For more: Jean Dreze & Amartya Sen, *An Uncertain Glory: India and Its Contradictions* (Princeton: Princeton University Press, 2013), Table A.3 in the Statistical Appendix.

[117] 'Economic Survey 2017', Government of Jammu and Kashmir: Directorate of Economics & Statistics, last accessed on 22 June 2020, http://ecostatjk.nic.in/publications/publications.htm

Past, Present, Future

[118] 542 out of the 543 constituencies went to poll in the 2019 General Election. Polling was cancelled in Vellore constituency because of electoral malpractice, after millions of rupees in cash were unearthed in an income tax raid from a candidate's house.

[119] 'Lok Sabha elections 2019: Performance of National Parties', Election Commission of India, last accessed on 23 June 2020, https://eci.gov.in/files/file/10955-20-performance-of-national-parties/

[120] 'Lok Sabha elections 2014: Performance of National Parties', Election Commission of India, last accessed on 23 June 2020, https://eci.gov.in/files/file/2820-performance-of-national-parties/

[121] Jyoti Mishra, 'CSDS-Lokniti pre-poll survey: the PM candidate effect', *The Hindu*, 20 May 2019, https://www.thehindu.com/elections/lok-sabha-2019/csds-lokniti-pre-poll-survey-the-pm-candidate-effect/article27189621.ece

[122] Micheal Safi, 'India election results 2019: Modi claims landslide victory', *The Guardian*, 23 May 2019, https://www.theguardian.com/world/2019/may/23/india-election-results-narendra-modi-bjp-victory

[123] India Today, 'Pulwama Attack: PM Modi Declares India's Intent, Gives Free Hand To Forces', YouTube, last accessed on 23 June 2020, https://www.youtube.com/watch?time_continue=110&v=UwJ75wFn25w&feature=emb_logo

[124] Sameer Yasir, 'Kashmir attack: Tracing the path that led to Pulwama', *BBC News*, 1 May 2019, https://www.bbc.com/news/world-asia-india-47302467

[125] Gaurav Vivek Bhatnagar, 'Youth Joining Militancy in Jammu and Kashmir on the Rise Since 2014, Says Home Ministry', *The Wire*, 21 March 2017, https://thewire.in/government/jammu-kashmir-militancy-infiltration

[126] Basharat Peer, *Curfewed Night* (Delhi: Penguin Books, 2009), 24–27.

[127] Nazir Masoodi, 'Attacks On Kashmiris After Pulwama Have Undone Years Of Hard Work', *NDTV*, 22 February 2019, https://

www.ndtv.com/blog/attacks-on-kashmiris-after-pulwama-have-undone-years-of-hard-work-1997806

[128] 'Pulwama attack: What is militant group Jaish-e-Mohammad?', *BBC News*, 15 February 2019, https://www.bbc.com/news/world-asia-47249982

[129] Nitin A. Gokhale, *The Inside Story of India's 2016 'Surgical Strikes'* (New Delhi: Bloomsbury, 2017), Excerpt published in *The Diplomat*, last accessed 23 June 2020, https://thediplomat.com/2017/09/the-inside-story-of-indias-2016-surgical-strikes/

[130] 'Lashkar-e-Tayyiba (LT)', *National Counterterrorism Centre*, Last accessed on 7 July 2020, https://www.dni.gov/nctc/groups/lt.html

[131] 'Mumbai train blasts: Death for five for 2006 bombings', *BBC News*, 30 September 2015, https://www.bbc.com/news/world-asia-india-34398810

[132] Praveen Swami, 'Uri attack: Jaish-e-Muhammad suspects in hand, evidence shown to envoy', *The Indian Express*, 4 October 2016, https://indianexpress.com/article/india/india-news-india/uri-attack-jaish-suspects-in-hand-evidence-shown-to-envoy-3053717/

[133] Praveen Swami, 'Surgical strikes: Bodies taken away on trucks, loud explosions, eyewitnesses give graphic details', *The Indian Express*, 7 October 2016, https://indianexpress.com/article/india/india-news-india/pakistan-border-terror-camps-surgical-strikes-kashmir-loc-indian-army-jihadist-3065975/

[134] M Ilyas Khan, 'India's "surgical strikes" in Kashmir: Truth or illusion?', *BBC News*, 23 October 2016, https://www.bbc.com/news/world-asia-india-37702790

[135] '"Someone justified his chest size today": Twitter cheers and chuckles after India's surgical strike', *Scroll*, 29 September 2016, https://scroll.in/article/817784/someone-justified-his-chest-size-today-twitter-cheers-and-chuckles-after-indias-surgical-strike

[136] During the 2014 elections campaign, Narendra Modi had said in reference to Samajwadi Party leader, Mulayam Singh Yadav's criticism that Modi cannot make another Gujarat out of Uttar Pradesh, 'Do you know it requires a 56-inch chest to make it'. The 56-inch chest has since then been used to refer to Modi's leadership style.

[137] Sakshi Parashar, 'India's Uri response: This is how Twitter reacted', *Economic Times*, 29 September 2016, https://economictimes. indiatimes.com/news/politics-and-nation/indias-uri-response-this-is-how-twitter-reacted/articleshow/54580509.cms

[138] Anita Katyal, 'Forced to eat its words, Congress hails Modi government for surgical strikes', *Scroll*, 29 September 2016, https:// scroll.in/article/817827/forced-to-eat-its-words-congress-hails-modi-government-for-surgical-strikes

[139] Vicky Kaushal(@vickykaushal9), 'What an honour! #WATCH: PM Modi asks "How's the josh?" at the inauguration of National Museum of Indian Cinema in Mumbai. The audience responds with 'High Sir', Twitter video, 19 January 2019, https://twitter.com/vickykaushal09/status/1086683536768155648

[140] '"How is the Jaish? Destroyed, sir": What front pages had to say about the IAF air strikes', *Scroll*, 27 February 2019, https://*scroll.in*/latest/914740/how-is-the-jaish-destroyed-sir-what-front-pages-had-to-say-about-the-iaf-air-strikes

[141] Fidayeen Jihadis is a term used in India to refer to Islamic militants who are ready to sacrifice their life for the cause of Jihad, commonly understood to imply that they become suicide bombers.

[142] 'Statement by Foreign Secretary on 26 February 2019 on the Strike on JeM training camp at Balakot', Ministry of External Affairs, 26 February 2019, https://www.mea.gov.in/press-releases. htm?dtl/31091/Statement_by_Foreign_Secretary_on_26_February_2019_on_the_Strike_on_JeM_training_camp_at_Balakot

[143] DG ISPR(@OfficialDGISPR), 'Indian aircrafts' intrusion across LoC in Muzafarabad Sector within AJ & K was 3-4 miles. Under forced hasty withdrawal aircrafts released payload which had free fall in open area. No infrastructure got hit, no casualties. Technical details and other important information to follow.', Twitter, 26 February 2019, https://twitter.com/OfficialDGISPR/status/1100251560985145346

[144] 'Balakot: Indian air strikes target militants in Pakistan', *BBC News*, 26 February 2019, https://www.bbc.com/news/world-asia-47366718

[145] DG ISPR(@OfficialDGISPR), 'In response to PAF strikes this morning as released by MoFA, IAF crossed LoC. PAF shot down two Indian aircrafts inside Pakistani airspace. One of the

aircraft fell inside AJ & K while other fell inside IOK. One Indian pilot arrested by troops on ground while two in the area.', Twitter, 27 February 2019, https://twitter.com/OfficialDGISPR/status/1100641491679150080

[146] Soutik Biswas, 'Narendra Modi v Imran Khan: Who won the war of perception?', *BBC News*, 1 March 2019, https://www.bbc.com/news/world-asia-india-47414490

[147] Govt of Pakistan(@pid_gov), 'Pakistan will release Indian Pilot Abhinandan tomorrow as a gesture of peace: Prime Minister Imran Khan', Twitter, 28 February 2019, https://twitter.com/pid_gov/status/1101077823987613697

[148] Simon Scarr, Chris Inton and Han Huang, 'An air strike and its aftermath', *Reuters*, 6 March 2019, https://graphics.reuters.com/INDIA-KASHMIR/010090XM162/index.html

[149] 'Annual Report 2018-19', Ministry of Home Affairs, last accessed on 25 June 2020, https://www.mha.gov.in/documents/annual-reports According to the Annual Report 2019-20 (accessed on 17 June 2021), there was a fall in the number of terrorists killed (157) and in the infiltration attempts (138) into the region in 2019.

Divided We Fall

[150] 'Clarifications on LoC', Ministry of External Affairs: Government of India, 2 July 1972, https://mea.gov.in/in-focus-article.htm?19004/Clarifications+on+LoC

[151] Pallavi Sareen, 'Army Veterans, Police Among Residents Attacked in Jammu City', *The Wire*, 18 February 2019, https://thewire.in/security/jammu-curfew-violence-pulwama-attack

[152] The website of Vishva Hindu Parishad states its objective as: 'The objective of the VHP is to organize—consolidate the Hindu society and to serve—protect the Hindu Dharma'. Critics call it a hard-line Hindu nationalist outfit, which is led by the ideologies of its parent organization, the Rashtriya Swayamsevak Sangh, that believes in the supremacy of Hindus and aims for a nation purged of non-Hindus.

[153] 'General Election, 1989 (Vol I, II)', Election Commission of India, last accessed on 8 July 2020, https://eci.gov.in/files/file/4120-general-election-1989-vol-i-ii/

[154] Christophe Jaffrelot, 'Ayodhya, the Babri Masjid and the Ramjanmabhoomi Dispute', in *Hindu Nationalism: A Reader*, ed. Christophe Jaffrelot (Ranikhet, Permanent Black, 2009). 281-282.

[155] Kaveree Bamzai, Harinder Baweja, Dilip Awasthi, 'BJP flag-hoisting ceremony in Srinagar turns out to be a damp squib, militancy gets a boost', *India Today*, 15 February 1992, https://www.indiatoday.in/magazine/special-report/story/19920215-bjp-flag-hoisting-ceremony-in-srinagar-turns-out-to-be-a-damp-squib-militancy-gets-a-boost-765818-2013-06-24

[156] 'Constituency Maps', Chief Electoral Officer: UT of Jammu and Kashmir and Ladakh, last accessed on 25 June 2020, http://ceojammukashmir.nic.in/Constituency_Maps.htm

[157] Sameer Yasir, 'The child rape and murder that has Kashmir on edge', *BBC News*, 12 April 2018, https://www.bbc.com/news/world-asia-india-43722714

[158] Press Trust of India, 'Jammu and Kashmir Registers Highest Voter Turnout in 25 Years, Jharkhand Breaks Records', *NDTV*, 21 December 2014, https://www.ndtv.com/assembly/jammu-and-kashmir-registers-highest-voter-turnout-in-25-years-jharkhand-breaks-records-715845

[159] Press Trust of India, 'Big win for BJP in Jammu; bags 25 of 37 seats', *DNA*, 23 December 2014, https://www.dnaindia.com/india/report-big-win-for-bjp-in-jammu-bags-25-of-37-seats-2046564

[160] 'Self-Rule Framework', Jammu and Kashmir Peoples Democratic Party, last accessed on 26 June 2020, https://web.archive.org/web/20140109142821/http://jkpdp.org/self-rule/self-rule-framework/

[161] 'BJP ends its Jammu and Kashmir alliance with PDP, cites national interest, security slide', *Financial Express*, 20 June 2018, https://www.financialexpress.com/india-news/bjp-ends-its-jammu-and-kashmir-alliance-with-pdp-cites-national-interest-security-slide/1212594/

[162] Yashwant Sinha, Wajahat Habibullah, Kapil Kak, Bharat Bhushan and Sushobha Barve, 'Ceasefire Revocation, Shujaat Bukhari's Murder, the BJP-PDP Split: What Kashmir Thinks—A report by the Concerned Citizens' Group following their visit to Srinagar', *The Wire*, 2 July 2018, https://thewire.in/politics/ramzan-ceasefir-shujaat-bukhari-bjp-pdp-kashmir

[163] Liz Matthew, 'Here's why the BJP dumped the PDP, and it has nothing to do with terror', *The Indian Express*, 20 June 2018, https://indianexpress.com/article/india/heres-why-the-bjp-dumped-the-pdp-and-it-has-nothing-to-do-with-terror/

[164] Press Trust of India, 'BJP ministers who took part in rally in support of Kathua rape case accused submit resignation', *The Economic Times*, 14 April 2018, https://economictimes.indiatimes.com/news/politics-and-nation/kathua-rape-two-bjp-cabinet-ministers-quit/articleshow/63752377.cms

[165] Rifat Fareed, 'Panic in Kashmir after India asks tourists and pilgrims to leave', *Al-Jazeera*, 3 August 2019, https://www.aljazeera.com/news/2019/08/panic-kashmir-india-asks-tourists-pilgrims-leave-190802145955424.html

[166] Azaan Javaid, 'J & K Governor & state BJP dispel Article 35A rumours, party says troop movement is for polls', *The Print*, 30 July 2019, https://theprint.in/india/jk-governor-state-bjp-dispel-article-35a-rumours-party-says-troop-movement-is-for-polls/270094/

[167] ANI(@ANI), 'J & K govt issues security advisory in the interest of #AmarnathYatra pilgrims and tourists, "that they may curtail their stay in the Valley immediately and take necessary measures to return as soon as possible", keeping in view the latest intelligence inputs of terror threats.', Twitter photo, 2 August 2019, https://twitter.com/ANI/status/1157235503256805378

[168] Smita Sharma (@Smita_Sharma), 'UK issues advisory for its nationals against all travel to #Jammu #Kashmir https://gov.uk/foreign-travel-advice/india/safety-and-security "There is a risk of unpredictable violence, including bombings, grenade attacks, shootings and kidnapping" says fresh advisory, @UKinIndia @HCI_London @MEAIndia @PIBHomeAffairs', Twitter photo, 3 August 2019, https://twitter.com/Smita_Sharma/status/1157597122251784192

[169] Mehbooba Mufti (@MehboobaMufti), 'In such difficult times, I'd like to assure our people that come what may, we are in this together & will fight it out. Nothing should break our resolve to strive for what's rightfully ours.', 4 August 2019, https://twitter.com/MehboobaMufti/status/1158076327477444608

[170] Omar Abdullah (@OmarAbdullah), 'I believe I'm being placed under house arrest from midnight tonight & the process has already started for other mainstream leaders. No way of knowing if this is true but if it is then I'll see all of you on the other side of whatever is in store. Allah save us', Twitter, 4 August 2019, https://twitter.com/OmarAbdullah/status/1158075327333031941

[171] Spriha Srivastava, 'India revokes special status for Kashmir. Here's what it means', *Al-Jazeera*, 5 August 2019, https://www.cnbc.com/2019/08/05/article-370-what-is-happening-in-kashmir-india-revokes-special-status.html

[172] Bilal Kuchay, 'India: The main takeaways from BJP's manifesto', *Al-Jazeera*, 8 April 2019, https://www.aljazeera.com/news/2019/04/india-main-takeaways-bjp-manifesto-190408121132327.html

India

[173] Aamir Peerzada, 'What did change in Kashmir within 24 hours', BBC Hindi on Facebook, 6 August 2019, https://www.facebook.com/watch/?v=323755188318267

[174] Ramachandra Guha, *India After Gandhi: The History of the World's Largest Democracy* (London: Pan Macmillan, 2007), 248-254.

[175] 'The Constitution (Application to Jammu and Kashmir) Order, 1954', Government of Jammu and Kashmir: Department of Law, Justice & Parliamentary Affairs, last accessed 29 June 2020, http://jklaw.nic.in/Constitution_jk.pdf

[176] 'The Constitution (Application to Jammu and Kashmir) Order, 2019', *The Gazette of India*, last accessed 29 June 2020, http://egazette.nic.in/WriteReadData/2019/210049.pdf

[177] 'Government abolishes Article 370, massive uproar in House', *Economic Times*, 5 August 2019, https://economictimes.indiatimes.com/news/politics-and-nation/government-abolishes-article-370-massive-opposition-uproar-in-house/articleshow/70533966.cms

[178] 'Article 370: Constitution bench to hear matter. Timeline of what has happened in SC so far', *India Today*, 28 August 2019, https://www.indiatoday.in/india/story/article-370-case-Constitution-bench-timeline-supreme-court-1592505-2019-08-28

[179] 'PM Modi addresses the nation', narendramodi.in, 8 August 2019, https://www.narendramodi.in/prime-minister-narendra-modi-s-address-to-the-nation-on-8th-august-2019-545901

[180] Betwa Sharma, 'In Jammu, Hindus Are "Confused", Worried About Article 370, But Won't Speak Out', *Huffington Post*, 25 October 2019, https://www.huffingtonpost.in/entry/jammu-kashmir-hindus-article-370-union-territory_in_5db156a6e4b0131fa999b772

[181] BBC News, 'Tear gas at Kashmir rally India denies happened', YouTube, 10 August 2019, https://www.youtube.com/watch?v=Nica1EKi2h8

[182] 'Indian troops fire tear gas as mass protests erupt in Srinagar', *Al Jazeera*, 9 August 2019, https://www.aljazeera.com/news/2019/08/indian-troops-fire-tear-gas-mass-protests-erupt-srinagar-190809151858216.html

[183] Devjyot Ghoshal, Fayaz Bukhari, 'Thousands protest in Indian Kashmir over new status despite clampdown', *Reuters*, 9 August 2019, https://www.reuters.com/article/us-india-kashmir/thousands-protest-in-indian-kashmir-over-new-status-despite-clampdown-idUSKCN1UZ0OT

[184] 'Days after calling reports of unrest in Srinagar's Soura "fabricated", MHA admits to incident, but maintains no bullets were fired', *FirstPost*, 13 August 2019, https://www.firstpost.com/india/days-after-calling-reports-of-unrest-in-srinagars-soura-fabricated-mha-admits-to-incident-but-maintains-no-bullets-were-fired-7159101.html

[185] 'Kashmir Times editor moves Supreme Court seeking media freedom in Valley', *The Leaflet*, 10 August 2019, https://theleaflet.in/kashmir-times-editor-moves-supreme-court-seeking-media-freedom-in-Valley/

[186] 'Kashmir Live Updates: Owaisi slams clampdown, says emergency-like situation in Valley', *India Today*, 14 Augist 2019, https://www.indiatoday.in/india/story/kashmir-jammu-live-updates-supreme-court-hearing-article-370-1580220-2019-08-13

[187] Jean Drèze, Kavita Krishnan, Maimoona Mollah, Vimal Bhai, 'Kashmir Caged: A Fact Finding Report', National Confederation of Human Rights Organizations, 14 August 2019, https://www.nchro.

org/index.php/2019/08/14/kashmir-caged-a-fact-finding-report-by-jean-dreze-kavita-krishnan-maimoona-mollah-and-vimal-bhai/

[188] Aamir Peerzada, Neha Sharma, 'Search for answers over Kashmir detentions', *BBC News*, 23 August 2019, https://www.bbc.com/news/av/world-asia-49448138

[189] Devjyot Ghoshal, Alasdair Pal, 'Thousands detained in Indian Kashmir crackdown, official data reveals', *Reuters*, 20 September 2019, https://in.reuters.com/article/india-kashmir-detentions/thousands-detained-in-indian-kashmir-crackdown-official-data-reveals-idINKCN1VX12W

[190] Sameer Hashmi, '"Don't beat us, just shoot us": Kashmiris allege violent army crackdown', *BBC News*, 29 August 2019, https://www.bbc.com/news/world-asia-india-49481180

[191] Shaswati Das, 'Post-Article 370's revocation, Kashmir observes first Independence Day amid curfew', *LiveMint*, 16 August 2019, https://www.livemint.com/politics/news/post-article-370-s-revocation-kashmir-observes-first-independence-day-amid-curfew-1565893377220.html

[192] Indo Asian News Service, 'Schools reopen in Srinagar, but students missing', *Outlook India*, 19 August 2019, https://www.outlookindia.com/newsscroll/schools-reopen-in-srinagar-but-students-missing/1599530

[193] Naina Bajekal, 'India Is Slowly Easing Its Lockdown in Kashmir. But Life Isn't Returning to Normal', *Time*, 23 October 2019, https://time.com/5706847/what-happens-now-kashmir/

[194] Aamir Peerzada, 'Kashmir aur Ladakh main kaise paanv pasaar rahi hai BJP' (How is the BJP expanding its network in Kashmir and Ladakh), *BBC Hindi*, 20 November 2019, https://www.bbc.com/hindi/india-50483712

Rebellions

[195] Ministry of Law and Justice, 'The Citizenship (Amendment) Act 2019', *The Gazette of India*, 12 December 2019, http://egazette.nic.in/WriteReadData/2019/214646.pdf

[196] 'National Register of Citizens (NRC)', Government of Assam, last accessed on 1 July 2020, https://assam.gov.in/en/main/NRC

[197] Sangeeta Barooah Pisharoty, 'Women Without Parents: An NRC Ground Report', *The Wire*, 13 September 2019, https://thewire.in/rights/women-without-parents-an-nrc-ground-report

[198] Shaswati Das, 'NRC will be rolled out across the country before 2024 polls: Amit Shah', *Live Mint*, 3 December 2019, https://www.livemint.com/news/india/nationwide-nrc-to-be-implemented-before-2024-lok-sabha-polls-amit-shah-11575290024624.html

[199] Vijayta Lalwani, 'Meet the brave women of Jamia who rescued a fellow student from the clutches of Delhi Police', *Scroll*, 16 December 2019, https://scroll.in/article/947026/meet-the-brave-women-of-jamia-who-rescued-a-fellow-student-from-the-clutches-of-delhi-police

[200] Nehal Ahmed & Grace Raju, '"We heard gunfire": Jamia students detail police attack on campus', *Al Jazeera*, 18 December 2019, https://www.aljazeera.com/news/2019/12/heard-gunfire-jamia-students-detail-police-attack-campus-191218063347967.html

[201] Vatsala Gaur, 'After Jamia, Police uses brute force to quell protests at AMU', *Economic Times*, 15 December 2019, https://economictimes.indiatimes.com/news/politics-and-nation/amu-students-protest-against-caa-cops-use-batons-teargas/articleshow/72697984.cms?from=mdr

[202] Narendra Modi (@narendramodi), 'I want to unequivocally assure my fellow Indians that CAA does not affect any citizen of India of any religion. No Indian has anything to worry regarding this Act. This Act is only for those who have faced years of persecution outside and have no other place to go except India.', Twitter, 16 December 2019, https://twitter.com/narendramodi/status/1206492850378002432

[203] narendramodi_in (@narendramodi_in), '#IndiaSupportsCAA because CAA is about giving citizenship to persecuted refugees & not about taking anyone's citizenship away. Check out this hashtag in Your Voice section of Volunteer module on NaMo App for content, graphics, videos & more. Share & show your support for CAA.', Twitter, 30 December 2019, https://twitter.com/narendramodi_in/status/1211517966228975617

[204] 'ABP-CVoter Survey On Citizenship Act: 62 percent Indians Support CAA, 65 percent Want Pan-India NRC Too', *ABP News*, 21 December 2019, https://news.abplive.com/news/india/abp-cvoter-

survey-on-citizenship-act-62-indians-support-caa-65-want-pan-india-nrc-too-1129900

[205] Ankur Pathak (@aktalkies), 'A phenomenal night at Mumbai's Carter Rd. The directors (Kashyap, Bhardwaj, Sinha, Akhtar) calmly directed, the singers and poets sang and recited, the actors (Richa, Taapsee, Dia, Swara, Ali) chimed in, the audiences watched and participated. Truly a Bombay blockbuster.', Twitter, 6 January 2020, https://twitter.com/aktalkies/status/1214229494392713216

[206] Sidharth Bhatia, '"PM Has Never Been a Student Himself, His Contempt For Them Is Not Surprising": Naseeruddin Shah', *The Wire*, 20 January 2020, https://thewire.in/film/naseeruddin-shah-interview-caa-communalism

[207] S. Irfan Habib (@irfhabib), 'Even this can happen in New India, police constables manhandling and arresting one of our most prolific and influential public intellectuals and scholars @Ram_Guha', Twitter, 19 December 2019, https://twitter.com/irfhabib/status/1207542945777209345

[208] Yogita Limaye (@yogital), 'Thread #India #UttarPradesh In Muzaffarnagar, a woman told us how her home had been vandalised by the police in the dead of the night. Their car, windows, mirrors, electronic appliances, crockery all broken. Jeweller, cash stolen.', Twitter, 27 December 2019, https://twitter.com/yogital/status/1210514405730873345

[209] Kumar Abhishek, 'CAA protests: UP government starts process to seize property of protesters involved in violence', *India Today*, 22 December 2019, https://www.indiatoday.in/india/story/caa-protests-up-government-starts-process-seize-property-protesters-involved-violence-1630471-2019-12-22

[210] Chinki Sinha, 'CAA: Muslim ladkiyon ka aanchal bana parcham, kya hain iske maayne?' (CAA: What is the significance of Muslim women leading protests?), *BBC Hindi*, 6 January 2020, https://www.bbc.com/hindi/india-51000030

[211] Farah Naqvi, Sarojini N, Deepa V, Dipta Bhog, Malini Ghose, Shabani Hassanwalia, Jaya Sharma, Adsa Fatima, Disha Mullick, 'Unafraid: The Day Young Women Took the Battle to the Streets', *FeminisminIndia*, 27 December 2019, https://feminisminindia.com/wp-content/uploads/2019/12/Unafraid_271219_1730.pdf

212 Sanjay Kak, 'The last option : A stone in her hand', *The Times of India*, 8 August 2010, http://timesofindia.indiatimes.com/articleshow/6272689.cms?utm_source=contentofinterest&utm_medium=text&utm_campaign=cppst

213 Essar Batool, Ifrah Butt, Samreena Mushtaq, Munaza Rashid, Natasha Rather, *Do you remember Kunan-Poshpora?* (New Delhi: Zubaan, 2016), 6–7.

214 'Declaration on the Protection of All Persons from Enforced Disappearance', United Nations, 12 February 1993, https://undocs.org/A/RES/47/133

215 'A Provisional Biography of a Journey Towards Justice for the Enforced Disappeared', Association of Parents of Disappeared Persons, last accessed on 2 July 2020, https://apdpkashmir.com/a-provisional-biography-of-the-association-of-parents-of-disappeared-persons-kashmir/

216 'NHRC calls for report on the 'Disappearances' in the Kashmir Valley', National Human Rights Commission, last accessed on 2 July 2020, https://nhrc.nic.in/press-release/nhrc-calls-report-disappearances-kashmir-valley

217 Press Trust of India, 'Over 4000 terrorists, missing people of J & K in PoK: State government', *The Indian Express*, 16 January 2017, https://indianexpress.com/article/india/over-4000-terrorists-missing-people-of-jk-in-pok-state-government-4469475/

218 'Torture: Indian State's Instrument of Control in Indian administered Jammu and Kashmir', Association of Parents of Disappeared Persons (APDP) And Jammu Kashmir Coalition of Civil Society (JKCCS), February 2019, last accessed 2 July 2020, http://jkccs.net/wp-content/uploads/2019/05/TORTURE-Indian-State per centE2 per cent80 per cent99s-Instrument-of-Control-in-Indian-administered-Jammu-and-Kashmir.pdf

219 Mustafa Qureishi, '40-Feet Iron Structure of India's Map Installed at Shaheen Bagh', *The Quint*, 17 January 2020, https://www.thequint.com/news/india/40-ft-high-iron-structure-of-indias-map-installed-at-shaheen-bagh

220 'Fact Check: Has Government Always Denied NPR-NRC Link?', *Outlook*, 25 December 2019, https://www.outlookindia.com/website/

story/india-news-fact-check-has-government-always-denied-npr-nrc-link/344665

221 Asim Ali, 'Foolish to think Hindus who voted Modi twice will shift due to threat to Muslim citizenship', *The Print*, 2 January 2020, https://theprint.in/opinion/foolish-to-think-hindus-who-voted-modi-twice-will-shift-due-to-threat-to-muslim-citizenship/343569/

222 'JNU violence: Students recount attack by a masked mob, said Delhi Police watched', *The Caravan*, 6 January 2020, https://caravanmagazine.in/education/jnu-abvp-attack-5-january

223 Times Now, '#JNUHiddenTruth Listen in: ABVP Delhi State Jt Secretary "explains" the video of alleged ABVP violence in JNU. @thenewshour Agenda with Padmaja Joshi.', Twitter, 6 January 2020, https://twitter.com/TimesNow/status/1214229897717010433

224 Press Trust of India, 'Hindu Raksha Dal claims responsibility for JNU attack', *The Times of India*, 7 January 2020, https://m.timesofindia.com/india/hindu-raksha-dal-claims-responsibility-for-jnu-attack/amp_articleshow/73137267.cms

225 Kai Shultz & Suhasini Raj, 'Behind Campus Attack in India, Some See a Far-Right Agenda', *The New York Times*, 10 January 2020, https://www.nytimes.com/2020/01/10/world/asia/india-jawaharlal-nehru-university-attack.html

226 'JNU protests: What is the hostel fee hike that students are protesting?', *The Indian Express*, 6 January 2020, https://indianexpress.com/article/explained/jnu-student-union-protest-fee-hike-jnusu-6114464/

Histories

227 Press Trust of India, 'Lt Guv seeks people's cooperation to build "new" J & K', *Outlook*, 25 January 2020, https://www.outlookindia.com/newsscroll/lt-guv-seeks-peoples-cooperation-to-build-new-jk/1717706

228 Press Trust of India, 'Republic Day 2020: Mobile phone, internet services snapped in Kashmir', *Business Standard*, 26 January 2020, https://www.business-standard.com/article/pti-stories/r-day-celebrations-mobile-phone-services-snapped-in-kashmir-120012600175_1.html

[229] Press Trust of India, 'Ahead of Republic Day parade, Jammu and Kashmir removes word "Sher-e-Kashmir" from name of gallantry and police medals', *Firstpost*, 26 January 2020, https://www.firstpost.com/india/ahead-of-republic-day-parade-jammu-and-kashmir-removes-word-sher-e-kashmir-from-name-of-gallantry-and-police-medals-7957081.html

[230] Zulfikar Majid, 'Names of important institutions in J & K UT too be changed', *Deccan Herald*, 10 November 2019, https://www.deccanherald.com/national/north-and-central/names-of-important-institutions-in-jk-ut-to-be-changed-775063.html

[231] Zoya Hassan, 'Ayodhya: How Rajiv Gandhi's plan to use the Ram temple for the Congress party came undone', *Scroll*, 21 October 2019, https://scroll.in/article/941140/ayodhya-how-rajiv-gandhis-plan-to-use-the-ram-temple-for-the-congress-party-came-undone

[232] Nirupama Subramanian, 'Explained: The Kashmir Pandit tragedy', *The Indian Express*, 24 January 2020, https://indianexpress.com/article/explained/exodus-of-kashmiri-pandits-from-valley-6232410/

[233] Preface to *The Study Committee on Kashmir Affairs, BJP on Kashmir* (New Delhi: BJP Publications, 1995)

[234] Rahul Pandita, *Our Moon Has Blood Clots* (Noida: Random House India, 2013), 75–79.

[235] 'Demographics', Jammu and Kashmir Government, accessed 12 June 2020, https://jk.gov.in/jammukashmir/?q=demographics

[236] A Vaidyanathan, 'Supreme Court Refuses To Reopen 215 Cases In Kashmiri Pandits' Killings', *NDTV*, 24 July 2017, https://www.ndtv.com/india-news/supreme-court-refuses-to-reopen-215-cases-in-kashmiri-pandits-killings-1728500

[237] 'Supreme Court's Refusal To Reopen Cases Of Killings Of Kashmiri Pandits Disappointing', Amnesty International India, 28 October 2017, https://amnesty.org.in/news-update/supreme-courts-refusal-reopen-cases-killings-kashmiri-pandits-disappointing/

[238] Sumit Hakhoo, 'Kashmiri Pandits at crossroads of history', *The Tribune*, 19 January 2020, https://www.tribuneindia.com/news/j-k/kashmiri-pandits-at-crossroads-of-history-28316

[239] Shivam Vij, 'Why Kashmiri Pandits may never return to the Valley', *The Print*, 2 December 2019, https://theprint.in/opinion/why-kashmiri-pandits-may-never-return-to-the-valley/329103/

[240] Anmol Tikoo, 'What about the Kashmiri Pandits? Thirty Years Later, Make the Question Count', *The Wire*, 22 January 2020, https://thewire.in/rights/kashmiri-pandits-exile

[241] Ramachandra Guha, *India After Gandhi: The History of the World's Largest Democracy* (London: Pan Macmillan, 2007), 650-655.

[242] Vidhu Vinod Chopra Films, 'Mission Kashmir Official Trailer', YouTube, 19 November 2009, https://www.youtube.com/watch?v=dHXOdL7SMuA

[243] Arundhati Roy, *Listening to Grasshoppers: Field Notes on Democracy* (New Delhi: Penguin Books, 2009), 47–79.

[244] Dr M. Ashraf Bhatt, 'Bollywood's [Re]presentation of Kashmir And Kashmiri: From Romance (*Kashmir Ki Kali*) To Tragedy (*Haider*)', *Countercurrents*, 8 May 2015, https://www.countercurrents.org/bhat080515.htm

Postscript

[245] BBC Hindi, 'What did the girl from Kashmir write when it was under an internet shutdown?', YouTube, 5 March 2020, https://www.youtube.com/watch?v=X7l6dBhi3is

[246] 'Delhi riots: City tense after Hindu-Muslim clashes leave 27 dead', *BBC News*, 26 February 2020, https://www.bbc.com/news/world-asia-india-51639856

[247] 'Report of the DMC Fact-Finding Committee on North-East Delhi Riots of February 2020 Prepared for Delhi Minorities Commission' by the Fact-Finding Committee headed by Mr M.R. Shamshad Advocate-on-Record, Supreme Court of India, 27 June 2020, https://archive.org/details/dmc-delhi-riot-fact-report-2020

[248] Divya Arya (@divyaconnects), 'Minorities Minister @naqvimukhtar faces questions on #DelhiRiots , crackdown on dissent and the perception of their Government as anti-Muslim', Twitter, 30 July 2020, https://twitter.com/divyaconnects/status/1288677863483297793

[249] Rajshekhar, '17,000-page chargesheet filed against 15 for riots conspiracy', *The Times of India*, 17 September 2020, https://timesofindia.indiatimes.com/india/17000-page-chargesheet-filed-against-15-for-riots-conspiracy/articleshow/78158235.cms

[250] None of the laws passed by the different BJP-ruled states use the term 'Love Jihad': The Uttar Pradesh Prohibition of Unlawful Religious Conversion, The Madhya Pradesh Freedom of Religion Act, Uttarakhand Freedom of Religion Act and Gujarat Freedom of Religion (Amendment) Bill.

[251] Avantika Mehta, 'They Were Celebrating Their Special Day. Then Someone Cried "Love Jihad"', *Vice*, 21 December 2020, https://www.vice.com/en/article/epdaam/they-were-celebrating-their-special-day-then-someone-cried-love-jihad

[252] Hannah Ellis-Peterson, 'Muslims targeted under Indian state's "Love Jihad" law', *The Guardian*, 14 December 2020, https://www.theguardian.com/world/2020/dec/14/muslims-targeted-under-indian-states-love-jihad-law

[253] Asmita Nandy, 'Laws on Love Jihad? But Modi Govt, NCW Have No Data or Definition', *The Quint*, 19 November 2020, https://www.thequint.com/news/india/laws-on-love-jihad-but-modi-govt-ncw-have-no-data-or-definition#read-more

[254] Naseer Ganai, 'Kashmir Under Curfew Ahead Of First Anniversary Of Article 370 Abrogation', *Outlook India*, 3 August 2020, https://www.outlookindia.com/website/story/india-news-kashmir-to-be-under-curfew-ahead-of-first-anniversary-of-article-370-abrogation/357936

[255] 'India PM Modi lays foundation for Ayodhya Ram temple amid Covid surge', *BBC News*, 5 August 2020, https://www.bbc.com/news/world-asia-india-53577942

[256] 'Longest Shutdowns', Software Freedom Law Centre, https://internetshutdowns.in/, last accessed on 8 April 2021

[257] Order dated 10 January 2020 by the Hon'ble SC of India (WP No 1031 of 2019), https://main.sci.gov.in/supremecourt/2019/28817/28817_2019_2_1501_19350_Judgement_10-Jan-2020.pdf

[258] 'J & K: All restrictive orders to be reviewed in a week, says SC', *The Week*, 10 January 2020, https://www.theweek.in/news/india/2020/01/10/jammu-and-kashmir-article-370-restrictions-communication-curbs-ghulam-nabi-azad-anuradha-bhasin.html

[259] Kaunain Sheriff M, Bashaarat Masood, Naveed Iqbal, 'J & K: Most habeas corpus cases dragged on as court slammed govt on due process', *The Indian Express*, 4 August 2020, https://indianexpress.com/article/india/jammu-kashmir-article-370-habeas-corpus-detention-psa-6538085/

[260] Shruti Mahajan, 'Turning the clock back: How the Supreme Court has dealt with cases arising out of last year's abrogation of Article 370', *Bar and Bench*, 5 August 2020, https://www.barandbench.com/columns/supreme-court-dealt-with-cases-abrogation-of-article-370-jammu-and-kashmir

[261] Anees Zargar, '99 percent Habeas Corpus filed in J & K HC since August 2019 pending', 27 June 2020, *Newsclick*, https://www.newsclick.in/99 per cent25-Habeas-Corpus-Filed-Jammu-Kashmir-HC-August-2019-Pending

[262] Shreyas Narula & Shruti Rajgopalan, 'The Judicial Abrogation of Rights & Liberties In Kashmir', *Article14*, 25 September 2020, https://www.article-14.com/post/the-judicial-abrogation-of-rights-liberties-in-kashmir#:~:text=Another

[263] 'J & K: What is People's Alliance and Gupkar Declaration?', *The Times of India*, 24 October 2020, https://timesofindia.indiatimes.com/india/jk-what-is-peoples-alliance-gupkar-declaration/articleshow/78848440.cms

[264] Bhadra Sinha, 'A year & counting—clock ticking, but SC verdict yet awaited on over 20 pleas on Article 370 scrapping', *The Wire,* 3 January 2021, https://theprint.in/judiciary/a-year-counting-clock-ticking-but-sc-verdict-yet-awaited-on-over-20-pleas-on-article-370-scrapping/577946/

[265] 'Silence that halted political process in J-K', *The Kashmirwalla*, 9 February 2021, https://thekashmirwalla.com/2021/02/silence-that-halted-political-process-in-j-k/

[266] Mudasir Ahmad, 'A Brief History of the J & K Liberation Front, Now Banned Under UAPA', *The Wire*, 23 March 2019, https://thewire.in/security/kashmir-jklf-ban-yasin-malik

[267] Ravi Krishnan Khajuria, 'Court frames charges against Yasin Malik, nine others in 1989 kidnapping case', *Hindustan Times*, 30 January 2021, https://www.hindustantimes.com/india-news/court-frames-charges-against-yasin-malik-nine-others-in-1989-kidnapping-case-101611988361618.html

[268] Safwat Zargar, 'In Kashmir, leaders of the Jamaat-e-Islami are mystified by Centre's ban: "Our work is in the open"', *Scroll*, 2 March 2019, https://scroll.in/article/915117/in-kashmir-leaders-of-the-jamaat-e-islami-are-mystified-by-centres-ban-our-work-is-in-the-open

[269] Bashaarat Masood, 'Who was Riyaz Ahmad Naikoo, the Hizbul Mujahideen commander?', *The Indian Express*, 6 May 2020, https://indianexpress.com/article/explained/who-was-riyaz-ahmad-naikoo-hizbul-mujahideen-6396915/

[270] 'Violence-free DDC polls in J-K biggest achievement of our administration: Manoj Sinha', *ANI News*, 27 January 2021, https://www.aninews.in/news/national/general-news/violence-free-ddc-polls-in-j-k-biggest-achievement-of-our-administration-manoj-sinha20210127025418/

[271] Emily Schmall, 'Kashmir Votes, and India Hails It as Normalcy in a Dominated Region', *The New York Times*, 22 December 2020, https://www.nytimes.com/2020/12/22/world/asia/kashmir-modi-election.html

[272] Vijdan Mohammad Kawoosa, 'The Number Theory: Understanding the DDC elections results in Jammu and Kashmir', *Hindustan Times*, 24 December 2020, https://www.hindustantimes.com/india-news/the-number-theory-understanding-the-ddc-election-results-in-jammu-and-kashmir/story-JjJ6fMjzP2DXcn0LTMpM6H.html

[273] Hundreds of farmers have been camping outside Delhi's borders for months, some with their families, protesting against new farm laws brought in by the Central government under its agrarian reform policies, which they fear will lead to loss of livelihood.

ACKNOWLEDGEMENTS

Writing a book is like a finale, a curtain coming down. So first, to all that helped pick up a pen, form the ideas and begin.

To Rudra, for always believing in me. Always. Especially when I lose faith. For being rock solid and very flexible! For inspiring me to write and dream. For giving this book its title. And for helping us slow down and savour the life we have made together.

To my parents, for living their lives with humility, humanity and kindness. For teaching me to strive for that too. I try, partly succeed and then try harder. Their discipline and hard work have clarified that there are no shortcuts in life.

To my mom again, for making me a part of her world of the most feisty, strong and brave women. The Sahelis under the flyover, who asked me one of the most important questions when I turned eighteen—what did feminism mean to me? And the friends in Forum and Labia in Mumbai, for continuing to ask more questions when I was loaned to them. All of you made me a seeker.

To Silpa and Pooja, who feel like they have been around forever. For helping me make sense of myself and drowning me in unconditional love.

And second, to all who helped see this the light of day.

To Duaa's parents, Urfi Jan and Shabir Abdullah Bhat; and Saumya's parents, Bandna Sahi and Sanjiv Kumar. For believing in the project. Asking your daughters to open their hearts and minds. And for sharing that conversation.

To senior journalist Majid Jahangir, for being my friend in Kashmir. Always eager to help and willing to go out of his way.

To Kashif Siddiqui, for holding fort during my absence on that crucial first visit. And for intuitively finding the pictures, sound and texture that lift words off paper to tell their deeply felt story.

To BBC's Head of Indian Languages, Rupa Jha, who is always itching to push the envelope. Hers and ours. For encouraging me to find a human way to tell the stories of conflict. We need more editors like you.

To long-time India/South Asia correspondent Sanjoy Majumder who has been following Kashmir for decades. I am thankful for your sharp insights on the early drafts.

To BBC's Senior News Editor in London, Iain Haddow, for mentoring this baby. The book owes a lot to your considered feedback.

To Ramachandra Guha, Dominique Lapierre, Larry Collins, Christophe Jaffrelot, M.J. Akbar, Ajit Bhattacharjea, Kul Bhushan Mahotra, Basharat Peer, Rahul Pandita, Gauhar Gilani, Essar Batool, Ifrah Butt, Samreena Mushtaq, Munaza Rashid, Natasha Rather and to the many journalists who have fearlessly been telling the story of Kashmir and India. Your writings provided much needed context and empathy to unravel the layers that cloud popular understanding of the Kashmir conflict.

To my editor at Penguin, Sayoni Basu, for asking me to write. And for being patient.

And finally, to Abir, who I hope will grow up to find many such friendships in a more peaceful and forgiving world.

Divya Arya has been telling people's stories for almost two decades now. Navigating video, audio and text mediums across English and Hindi languages, she explores burning human rights and social justice issues with a gender lens. An award-winning journalist currently with the BBC, she has also presented the global news programme *OS* on BBC World Service radio from its London newsroom and launched the chat show *WorklifeIndia* on BBC World News TV from Delhi. Divya is the first journalist from India to be chosen as a Knight-Wallace Fellow at the University of Michigan. Her research was published in the collection of essays, *Breaching the Citadel*. She lives in Delhi.